CASE STUDIES IN

CULTURAL ANTHROPOLOGY

GENERAL EDITORS
George and Louise Spindler
STANFORD UNIVERSITY

———————

THE ISTHMUS ZAPOTECS

Southern Mexico (Isthmus Zapotec area shaded)

THE ISTHMUS ZAPOTECS

Women's Roles in Cultural Context

By

BEVERLY CHIÑAS

California State University, Chico

HOLT, RINEHART AND WINSTON, INC.

NEW YORK   CHICAGO   SAN FRANCISCO   ATLANTA

DALLAS   MONTREAL   TORONTO   LONDON   SYDNEY

Cover photo: *In Memoriam: A cherished friend, companion, and assistant.*

Library of Congress Cataloging in Publication Data

Chiñas, Beverly.
The Isthmus Zapotecs.

(Case Studies in cultural anthropology)
Bibliography: p.
1. Zapotec Indians—Social life and customs.
2. Indians of Mexico—Women.   I. Title.   II. Series.
(DNLM: 1. Anthropology, Cultural—Mexico.   2. Ethnology—Mexico.   3. Indians, North America.   4. Role.
5. Women.   F 1219.3.W6 C539i   1973)
F1221.Z3C46   301.41'2'09727   73-3945
ISBN: 0-03-080301-2

Foreword

About the Series

These case studies in cultural anthropology are designed to bring to students, in beginning and intermediate courses in the social sciences, insights into the richness and complexity of human life as it is lived in different ways and in different places. They are written by men and women who have lived in the societies they write about and who are professionally trained as observers and interpreters of human behavior. The authors are also teachers, and in writing their books they have kept the students who will read them foremost in their minds. It is our belief that when an understanding of ways of life very different from one's own is gained, abstractions and generalizations about social structure, cultural values, subsistence techniques, and the other universal categories of human social behavior become meaningful.

About the Author

Beverly Chiñas is Associate Professor of Anthropology at California State University, Chico, California. She received her M.A. degree in 1965 and her Ph.D. in 1968 from the University of California, Los Angeles. The fieldwork on which this case study is based was carried out during fifteen months in 1966–1967. Of her early life experiences, which led her to a career in anthropology, Dr. Chiñas states: "I was born and grew up on the Nebraska prairies which were then and still remain to a certain degree the Nebraska of Willa Cather. Having no playmates, I entertained myself with imaginary Indian children as fantasy companions while I roamed the hills and gullies of my father's ranch where Plains Indians had hunted bison less than a century earlier. Other peoples and other cultures have fascinated me since I first met them through the pages of the *National Geographic Magazine* before I could read. When I finished high school during World War II there was no chance for further education. I worked as a stenographer for several years, married, and began raising a family. I read everything I could find on history and anthropology and spent vacations year after year in the Southwest among the Navajos, Apaches, and Pueblo peoples. I wanted desperately to learn more. Secretly I entertained thoughts of undertaking college studies full-time, but it seemed so wildly impossible that I could not bring myself to discuss it with my family.

"When my daughter enrolled in kindergarten I finally found the courage to inquire about courses in anthropology at the local college. The next year I enrolled full-time, majoring in anthropology, but it was not until I received my B.A. and a scholarship to graduate school that I could bring myself to tell anyone outside my immediate family that I was doing anything more than 'taking a few courses at the college.'

"Having spent fifteen years of my life longing for an opportunity to advance my education, I find it very difficult to understand the 'turned off' students of today. I live, eat, sleep, and breathe anthropology, and my only regret is that I was not able to enter this engrossing profession earlier. I have always had and still retain very strong interest in creative writing, biology, geology, and ethology. Women's roles have been one of my great preoccupations since I became aware of some of the ambiguities of such roles in our culture, beginning about the age of twelve."

Dr. Chiñas presently teaches a course in women's roles crossculturally, as well as others concerning peasant cultures, economic anthropology, and Mesoamerican ethnology, and continues research among the Isthmus Zapotecs. Cooking, gardening, and hiking are her favorite diversions.

About the Book

This case study is written by a woman and stresses roles assigned on the basis of sex, with particular emphasis on women's roles. Beverly Chiñas, quite properly however, places this emphasis upon sex roles in the context of a wide-ranging descriptive analysis of salient features of Isthmus Zapotec culture.

As she points out, anthropological descriptions of cultures have been biased by the dominance of male anthropologists working through male informants in cultures where interaction between the sexes is subject to a great many restrictions. Many highly regarded ethnographies do indeed depict women as though they were a part of the background. The foreground is occupied by men carrying on public roles as hunters, head men, and honor seekers. Many reports, even some using sampling procedures, have failed to separate the sexes and the data relevant to each. In our research with the Menomini and the Blood Indians, and in our current work in Germany, we have found it to be imperative to treat males and females as representing two potentially quite different universes. As Dr. Chiñas points out, other anthropologists have found this to be of critical importance as well.

Her model for the analysis of sex roles emphasizes the distinction between formalized and nonformalized roles. She correctly regards the formalized roles as constituting the most visible, but quantitatively the smallest, part of the total role structure of the cultural system. The formalized roles, which are most often occupied by men, particularly in their public dimensions, have been most frequently described because they are manifest and because they are formalized. The nonformalized roles are frequently left unexplicated, thus giving a distorted perspective on the whole behavioral system and the complex of expectations and demands that lie behind behavior.

The reader will enjoy this case study not only because it has an interesting and relevant focus but also because it is lively in its descriptions and balanced in the treatment of various aspects of culture, including subsistence, life cycle, religion and ritual, social behavior, and relations to the changing social and cultural environment. It may be particularly interesting to the reader to become familiar with Michael Kearney's case study, *The Winds of Ixtepeji,* which centers on another Zapotec town in the state of Oaxaca. His focus is upon how people perceive reality and how such perceptions affect the conduct of village life. Though there are indeed differences between Zapotecan communities, there is a commonality of culture. The emphases of two anthropologists working within a common cultural frame of reference, though in different communities, are, in these cases, complementary to each other and together provide the potential for a relatively complete understanding of this important cultural type.

LOUISE AND GEORGE SPINDLER
General Editors

Stanford, California

Preface

For the anthropologist, the first major fieldwork experience is akin to the initiation rites which young people in nonliterate cultures must often "pass" in order to become adults. The "elders" have prepared the budding anthropologist as best they could in classroom, seminar, and simulated or limited field experiences near at hand. Finally, the novitiate conceives and designs a research project and presents it to a fund-granting institution. Providing the institution considers his project worthy and funds are available, the initiate eventually finds himself actually "in the field" ready to begin the first major undertaking of his career.

In my case "the field" was the Isthmus of Tehuantepec, Mexico. As is usually the case, I arrived there uninvited, unannounced, and unexpected, as naive as a child concerning the correct modes of behavior in Zapotec culture. Although I spoke and understood Spanish, I was totally unfamiliar with Zapotec, the first language of most of the inhabitants. Since more than half the population were bilingual, it was my plan not to spend months learning Zapotec but rather to hire a bilingual local person as interpreter when needed.

The first couple of weeks passed quickly. I sought out important local persons such as the *presidente* of the town, introducing myself, explaining my project, and asking for cooperation. I looked for suitable quarters where I could both live and work with relative efficiency at the rather formidable task of recording, organizing, and analyzing field notes and data as accumulated. Because my project centered around women's market activities, I spent considerable time loitering in the several markets of the region, at first mainly observing since I had not yet obtained enough information to formulate the questions I eventually wished to ask. The Isthmus dialect of Spanish is so heavily laced with Zapotec intonation and phraseology that I initially found it difficult to understand, but that situation improved rapidly. I succeeded in finding a spacious house only a couple of blocks from the main marketplace, where I signed a three-month lease, although the rent was triple the amount I had budgeted from my modest living allowance.

The size of the marketplace in El Centro[1] seemed more amenable to the research efforts of a lone fieldworker than that of neighboring San Jacinto, and this fact plus convenient quarters led to my decision to concentrate my efforts in El Centro. On the other hand, it is doubtful that I could have found a more unpleasant, malodorous marketplace in all of Mexico.[2] The main structure, purported to date

---

[1] Throughout the case study place names are changed where it is necessary to protect the privacy of informants. Fictitious names are substituted for all persons, except historical personages, for the same reason. Words which appear in the glossary are italicized only the first time they are used.

[2] An informant's letter just received indicates that a new market structure has recently been started.

from the 1840s, was buried in the heart of a patchwork of annexes, arcades, expansions, and alterations which had been accomplished at various times over more than a century. The result was a cavernous interior with incredibly poor light and ventilation, crowded with two or three hundred women vendors and customers and a rather astonishing array of fresh and decaying produce, flowers, meat, fish, and poultry, as well as every description of nonperishable food product, yard goods, clothing, housewares, and hardware. The combinations of scents which greeted the unwary market entrant were at first so overwhelming as to prove nauseating. But I soon struck upon a game which served to divert my attention upon entrance until I became accustomed to the unfamiliar odors. The "game" was nothing more than trying to distinguish the individual sources of the various intermingled odors, some of which were most agreeable when considered singly.

During the first weeks I familiarized myself with the names of products and their sources, an activity that seemed innocuous and was easily elicited from the women vendors. I spent a couple of weeks mapping the interior of the main marketplace and its outdoor annex. Reports had led me to anticipate a considerable degree of suspicion and hostility, but these failed to materialize at first. People apparently assumed that I was only a curious *turista* who would soon disappear. When that did not occur and I began sketching the market's layout, people began to display increasing curiosity about my motives. I answered all questions as truthfully and comprehensibly as possible. I was making a study of the Isthmus markets, the products bought and sold, the sources of products, and characteristics of the vendors for the purpose of writing a *tesis* as part of my training to be a teacher. This was understandable to some persons at least, except for the fact that I, a "rich *Gringa,*" had come all the way from my country, alone, to study such a poor, simple thing. The word went around (without my knowledge at this point) that I was a spy. That was, after all, the only logical explanation for my continued presence and my preoccupation with the market place, its activities, and personnel. I was a spy "for the government," sent to gather information for the purpose of increasing taxes! It was not long before a few women refused to answer my questions. More women joined them. In a very few days the general attitude of the market place was hostile, even though two or three women continued to be very cooperative and friendly and tried to smooth out the difficulties on my behalf. The male guard asked if I had permission to ask questions. I produced the letter of introduction from the presidente. The guard, looking precisely like the sinister *soldado* of Mexican western films, spat on the floor and said my letter was worthless. There was now a new presidente and I would have to obtain *his* permission.[3]

Since I had the support of a few people, I thought it best to try to weather the storm. Doggedly each morning I entered the marketplace with a bright (and certainly forced) smile. Just as doggedly my most vocal adversary, an elderly *señora* whom I am sure thought she was doing a great service to her people, mounted the counter of her *puesto* and began her long and loud harangue against me. When conditions did not improve within a few days, I decided my temporary absence

---

[3] The first presidente, I learned, was only an interim official appointed by the governor to fill the office until a disputed election was settled.

might lower the anxiety level which continued to build among the market vendors. The time could be well spent making a survey of a number of marketplaces in Oaxaca, Chiapas, and Veracruz.

In my absence the spy story hit the front page of a regional weekly. I was now reported to be a "Yankee imperialist" spy whose government had a vital interest in the region as the site of a new interocean canal! The reporter suggested that immigration authorities might be interested in my case and that I would probably be deported henceforth. Fortunately the spy story had already run its course by the time I returned, and I was gradually able to resume work in the marketplace. Eventually I obtained the cooperation of most of the previously hostile women, some of whom later apologized for their discourteous treatment and invited me to visit them in their homes.

Soon after my first visits to the marketplace, I discovered that buying a small quantity of some unfamiliar food item and then striking up a conversation about it with the vendor was a pleasant way of establishing rapport. I continued this practice as I resumed work after the "spy scare." Often the purchase was something I could share with the women themselves, several of us sampling the food together on the spot. A favorite place of the *tortilleras* was around the perimeter of the venerable central fountain, which served as the only source of potable water for the entire marketplace. One morning after sampling a bit of fried dough, which I had shared with two tortilleras, I casually bent over and dipped my fingertips in the bottom basin of the fountain. A dozen loud voices protested, catching me completely by surprise. I must have looked as puzzled as I felt when I asked the woman beside me what I had done wrong. "You washed your hand in the fountain and that's bad. That is the water we use for cooking and washing dishes." Properly humiliated, I made my apologies, explaining that I would certainly abide by all the rules if known to me. The women smiled and began talking, asking me questions about my family, my home, my clothing, and my country. That small incident changed the tenor of my relationship with the market women. It occurred to me that at least I would never have to worry about Isthmus Zapotec women laughing at my mistakes behind my back as is the case in some cultures. No, indeed. These women, one could be certain, would point out my mistakes immediately and directly. Their candor and frankness were surely among their most enchanting and refreshing characteristics. Rapport with the women improved steadily thereafter as I assumed the role of naive student of *las costumbres* (not at all a difficult role at this point) and they were placed in the more rewarding role of teacher.

But if relations with the women improved, there were other problems that continued to plague me to the end. One of these was obtaining official data and information, as the following excerpt from my daily record indicates:

3-3-67. Went to El Centro at 8 A.M. First went to Palacio. I told secretary Romero: "Well, this is the day I was to return." "Oh, what may I do for you, señorita?" "Do you have the census data?" "Census? No, but I can order the book from the library for you ahorita." "No, señor, it's the census data that the maestros and students collected last month that I need." "Oh, did they make a census?" (That after he had promised a week ago to get it for me pronto!) "Yes, Señor Romero, they did and I understood that your office had the data."

"No, señorita, I don't know anything about it but let me talk to the director of the school." "Thank you, Sr. Romero, but that's not necessary. I can speak to him on my way home." (Director wasn't in.) After six months I am still waiting for the first delivery of any promised data from anyone!

This afternoon I went to house of Maestro Muñoz who had promised census data for San Juan Evangelista a month ago. He wasn't there but same old story. His wife said: "Oh, was there a census?????" I told her I could pay for whatever time was required to get the information. "But it's very easy. It only takes a few minutes. It isn't necessary to pay." We visited for an hour. Maestro Muñoz didn't arrive. . . .

Frustrations there were, but there were almost humorous situations and those which seem more humorous in retrospect. For example, this terse note from my daily record:

Saturday, 2-4-67. As promised I took Bilma and Panchita to *el campo*. All the Gallegos children, another girl, and a couple of miscellaneous niños went along (not as planned). I hit a bad hole and Roberto's head broke the camper window but his head is intact. This is the last time children ride in the back! Bilma told me her huertas were very near, right by the cemetery. They are five miles away. She said the road was good (it is barely passable). In addition I foolishly didn't wear slacks and am covered with sancudo bites.

Or the following, recorded as part of a visit to the sick mother of a friend:

1-17-67. I was feeling pretty good this P.M. so I went over to Xadani to see when Aurelia wanted to go to Tabasco. . . . The conversation turned to curing. Chica said she heard there's a *gringa* who lives in Mixtequilla, who prescribes the two hind legs of a cricket be put in the bed with the patient to cure backache and she thought they should try it for her mother. I asked if she needed crickets (I have plenty) but she said no, she had *un montón* at her house too. Don't suppose anyone would be interested in several hundred bats or a couple of fat iguanas either!

When my three-month lease expired, the most urgent work in the central marketplace was completed. I wanted to become more intimately involved in neighborhood life in order to gain a better understanding of family, kin, and neighborhood social interrelationships. I rented a smaller but comfortable house just at the entrance to San Juan Evangelista, where most of the traffic entering and leaving the pueblo, mainly afoot, passed my door. Slowly over the months that followed I learned something of the ways of Isthmus Zapotec culture with the help and guidance of a great many kind and patient "teachers." I patterned my actions and responses as closely after my neighbors as possible. At first I played the new roles consciously and superficially. Especially in ritual situations—wedding fiestas, funeral rites, fiestas to the saints, and such—where expected behavior was completely unfamiliar to me, I carefully followed the women's behavior patterns. When they knelt, I knelt, when they prayed, I tried to pray in the same words, and when they paid their *limosnas*, I did likewise. Gradually the correct responses, the expected behavior, began to become internalized and automatic in many situations. Before I left my many good friends and my adopted family at San Juan Evangelista, I felt I was at least a small part of the way toward becoming a *Juaneca*.

The people permitted me to share with them many hours of dull routine (which was seldom dull for me), as well as moments of intense joy, sorrow, and despair. A few individuals selflessly came to share my own hopes, confidences, and small moments of triumph and defeat. Those many hours of listening and talking, the unstructured research one does simply by living with people, were among the most informative and rewarding of all. I hope my Zapotec friends remember those times with equal pleasure.

I went to the Isthmus as a stranger, but a stranger I shall never be there again. On the two occasions since 1967 when I have returned to visit, someone has soon welcomed me with "Ay, Bévi, ¡Que milagro! You've come home." It is a sentiment I cherish and proudly share.

Acknowledgments

It would be impossible to thank each of the many individuals to whom I owe much for help in fieldwork and in completing this case study. The initial fieldwork could not have been undertaken without the generous assistance of the National Science Foundation (GN 1064). Especially profound is my debt to Ralph L. Beals of the University of California, Los Angeles, who encouraged me in the formulation of the original research project and offered advice and moral support throughout. I am also indebted to George M. Foster of the University of California, Berkeley, for his helpful comments from time to time when the case study was in the planning stages, and especially for his reading and advice on the original case-study outline. My colleagues at California State University, Chico, have graciously and patiently acted as a sounding board and have unfailingly given of their time and their support. Students have provided their own unique form of support in their enthusiasm and interest in my fieldwork and in Isthmus Zapotec culture.

To my friends in the Isthmus of Tehuantepec, for their graciousness as my hosts and teachers, this case study is an inadequate but sincere expression of my great admiration and gratitude. Although I cannot identify them individually, many will recognize themselves in the pages that follow. My deepest debt is to my dear friends, Doña Dolores and Conchita. Their trust, empathy, and intelligent assistance, so generously and selflessly given, are responsible in large measure for whatever insight I was able to gain into life in San Juan Evangelista. ¡Que Diós les quiera!

Chico, California
May 1973

BEVERLY CHIÑAS

Contents

THE ISTHMUS ZAPOTECS

Introduction

Anthropologists have usually described the cultures they study by focusing on men and men's roles, not particularly because anyone planned it that way but rather because such an orientation was the logical outcome of male anthropologists working through male informants in cultures where interaction between the sexes is subject to a great many restrictions, prescriptions, and taboos. In *The Isthmus Zapotecs* I try to reverse this time-honored tradition, not because I believe women are more important than men in Isthmus Zapotec culture but because it seems to me as valid a focal point as its counterpart and one too long neglected. *The Isthmus Zapotecs* is not a study only of the women but of a cultural system and women's roles within it. My goal is to present the reader with an image of the ways in which the roles of the sexes are mutually dependent and complementary in terms of everyday living, not only in the economic division of labor but in every aspect of the social system.

Since anthropologists research and analyze whole cultures (the holistic approach) and women are part of the whole, they have always been included in anthropology to some extent. Too often, however, women are presented ethnographically in a curiously impersonal, dehumanizing way—as shadows moving in and out of the important and engrossing activities of men or as objects whose main functions are to serve and to be manipulated by their menfolk (fathers, brothers, husbands, and sons). The women seem to be passive, mindless creatures as colorless as fog. If ever such a presentation reflects women's views of their culture, it must certainly be the rare exception. Probably more than a little of our own cultural bias is involved. The same emphasis on men and male activities can be viewed nightly on the national television networks, appearing perhaps in its purest form in the ubiquitous western.

Focusing on male roles in other cultures is not confined to male anthropologists of course. Women anthropologists have often done likewise, selecting field problems which center around male roles in the first place because, as a friend recently explained it, "that's where the action is." The truth of her statement undoubtedly lies in how one chooses to define "action," yet whatever the answer, the fact remains that women as culture bearers and as approximately one half of the participants in every culture deserve more attention than they have generally received if we are to gain an adequate understanding of that enormously complex whole we call culture.

Part of the problem of dealing effectively with women's roles has surely been the tendency to evaluate them in terms of male roles. If one defines "action" in terms of what males do, then indeed male roles are "where the action is." Roles assigned on the basis of sex are often complementary and therefore not comparable. One of the first rules of logic teaches us that comparing things which are dissimilar leads to invalid conclusions. But where sex roles are concerned, the comparisons are too often implicit as are the assumptions derived from them. Perhaps we have overlooked the "action" of women's roles in many cultures because that action is qualitatively different from that associated with male roles.

Among the assumptions which appear to underlie too many ethnographic descriptions, two seem particularly crucial to the study of women's roles. The first assumption is that the sexes perceive their culture and their own sex's place in it in essentially the same way. The second assumption is that men and women share a common culture on similar terms. A number of anthropologists have suggested that such assumptions are almost surely invalid, varying perhaps in degree of invalidity from one culture to another. (See, for example, Elkin 1950; Friedl 1967; Mintz 1969, and Spindler and Spindler 1970.) For the great majority of anthropologists to date, however, sex roles have not attracted much interest. Recently a new generation of anthropologists with a keen interest in sex roles (or more properly, roles assigned on the basis of sex) has begun to address itself to a reexamination of the issue. The results of their efforts which are just beginning to be reported at professional conferences and in professional journals should contribute much to our knowledge of sex roles and their variations crossculturally. It is my hope that *The Isthmus Zapotecs* can make a contribution to our inchoate body of such knowledge.

Turning attention to the case study, one of the most difficult tasks has been to describe Isthmus Zapotec culture briefly but in sufficient detail to convey an accurate image of the culture and the people. A culture presents many images, all of which may be equally accurate, but none of which taken alone describes the culture. Every anthropologist is forced to discriminate and select, both in recording his data and in reporting. What I report here is only a part of Isthmus Zapotec culture. If it is not that part which my many Zapotec friends and informants would have preferred, I offer apologies. Much of the cultural heritage of which they are so justly proud—their music, poetry, dances, traditional ceremonies, and their role in national history—has been recorded by others. A readable English language account of the region and the various ethnic populations of southern Mexico is *Mexico South* by Miguel Covarrubias, first published in 1946.

To facilitate an understanding of the part of Isthmus Zapotec culture reported in these pages, I employ two devices. The first is an analogy of the culture and its many strata to the earth viewed through a successive series of overlay maps. In the first overlay Isthmus Zapotec culture is perceived only superficially, in broad outline, somewhat analogous to viewing the earth's surface from an airplane at perhaps 5,000 feet elevation. As we proceed to subsequent levels of culture, different features are revealed at each level which allow us deeper insight into the culture just as peeling away pages of an overlay map of the earth would reveal different features of the earth's composition at each level. Limitations of time and space and knowledge allow us to view only a few of the cultural overlays. We leave to the reader the task of reintegrating in his own mind the various cultural levels presented. If I have done my job well, the reader should be able to "get the feel" of Isthmus Zapotec culture from these pages.

The second device is an analytical model of roles which I believe is useful for explaining and describing sex roles in Isthmus Zapotec culture. Role is here defined as the "bundle" of rights and duties associated with a particular status position. Every individual holds a number of statuses simultaneously and fills the roles associated with each status presumably to the best of his ability and understanding. But types of roles differ. Some are formalized to such an extent that every adult member of the social system knows the "bundle" of rights and duties the role demands even though he will never be expected to fill the role. Others are what I refer to as nonformalized, or roles which are not so clearly perceived or rigidly defined by members of the society. Perhaps we can conceptualize the totality of a social system as an iceberg, with the formalized roles representing the part which floats above the waterline, the visible part, and the nonformalized roles as the submerged but larger portion. The formalized roles lend themselves to description and analysis precisely because they are formalized. Thus these are most often the roles described by anthropologists and sociologists. Crosscutting the formalized-nonformalized dichotomy is another structural distinction which I shall refer to as private and public domains. The private domain refers to the basic social unit of the society, the family or other domestic group. The public domain refers to everything outside the basic social unit. This double dichotomy, formalized-nonformalized roles and private–public domains, yields four types of role distinction: (1) public formalized; (2) private formalized; (3) public nonformalized; and (4) private nonformalized.

Universally public formalized roles seem to be dominated by men. That is to say, the large majority of such roles are defined by the culture as male roles. Private formalized roles, on the other hand, usually seem to form complementary pairs by sex and are therefore often approximately equally divided between the sexes. Undoubtedly both sexes also function in many nonformalized roles, both public and private, but much less is known about these because they are not readily visible to the social scientists. Perhaps nonformalized roles outnumber formalized roles in all social systems, or perhaps there is much variation from one social system to the next. At present we simply do not know.

In Isthmus Zapotec culture, women often hold nonformalized complementary roles in the public sector for which men hold the formalized roles. To what degree this may be true universally is another unknown. Speaking only for the Isthmus Zapotec social system, knowledge of women's nonformalized roles appears to be as crucial to an understanding of the total system as is knowledge of the formalized roles of men.

Role distinctions in terms of the model are explained more fully in Chap. 8. First we must become familiar with the various cultural overlays, historical, ecological, and social, which form the background for Isthmus Zapotec role behavior. Here is the stage upon which the people of San Juan Evangelista interact as they seek to gain a livelihood, meet their familial, social, and religious obligations, and find some sense of personal satisfaction in their daily lives.

The aims of the case study are two: (1) to present a reflection of life in San Juan Evangelista which stresses the interdependency of the sexes and the complementary nature of their roles; and (2) to impart to the reader a sense of Isthmus Zapotec women's nonformalized roles and their importance to the social system.

1 / Wind, water, mountain, and plain: the physical setting

The Isthmus Zapotecs are the southern-most branch of a large population speaking several dialects of the indigenous language, Zapotec, and located in the state of Oaxaca, Mexico. Although the state is ethnically highly heterogeneous, Zapotec speakers have long been and remain the majority population of Oaxaca. Since pre-Contact times, 150 miles of rugged mountains have formed a barrier between the Isthmus Zapotecs and their linguistic cousins in the Valley of Oaxaca and in the *sierra*. This mountainous barrier has insulated more than isolated the Isthmus Zapotec population from the other Zapotec-speaking populations, so that the dialects have become mutually unintelligible for the most part and other cultural distinctions have evolved, mostly related to environment and subsistence patterns.

In national usage "El Istmo" refers only to the Pacific coastal plain of the geographical Isthmus of Tehuantepec, a usage followed throughout the case study because it defines the area of the Isthmus Zapotecs, an area occupied by the contemporary Zapotecs' ancestors for at least a thousand years.

The climate of El Istmo is tropical and semiarid by definition, although one gains the impression of severe desert-like aridity or lush verdancy, depending upon the season. The brief rainy season, late May through October, is marked by sudden torrential storms which cause a good deal of soil erosion and flooding. Although official records indicate that rainfall averaged 32 inches per year between 1956 and 1965, the nature of the rainfall and the porosity of the soil make effective rainfall considerably lower. Nonetheless, the rainy season is generally a pleasant time in El Istmo. Breezes freshen and become gentle, the inescapable dust is briefly stilled, and agricultural work lessens to the degree that water and mud make it impossible. With the first rains of the season yesterday's brown hills spring to life with tropical abandon, trees and bushes burst into flower, and roadsides turn velvet green. On fields without irrigation, crops have been carefully planted just before the rains to take full advantage of the short wet season. With luck, maize will be mature by the end of October when the rains cease. The violent wind, *el norte*, returns with the end of the rains, skittish and uncertain at first but soon ceaseless and raging, merciless in its onslaught for half the year.

Mother and daughter in yard of countryside home. (Dwelling to left is a choza.*)*

November and December are called the cold months by *Istmeños*, a time when one might need a sleeved garment or a light wool *robozo* in the early morning hours before dawn. Soon after the cessation of the rains the countryside is again brown and dead, the hills and *el monte* covered with spinous, xerophytic scrub interspersed with a few leafless deciduous trees. Starkness and desolation prevail, relieved only by the irrigated strips and splotches which remain lush through the long dry season, lending an oasis-like character to the landscape.

Since earliest occupation, two forces, wind and water, have molded Isthmus Zapotec subsistence patterns and culture. The destructive power of el norte has dictated the location of most Zapotec settlements behind or between the few hills which dot the coastal plain, affording a degree of protection from its relentless attack. Although native low-growing crops such as maize and cotton probably demanded minimal wind protection, the modern fruit crops of bananas and mangoes cannot be grown successfully except in the few microniches afforded by river valleys and the leeward side of the hills. This fact has led to a pattern of some intra-Isthmian agricultural specialization involving these fruits.

Water, however, has probably been more important to the people over the long run than has wind. There is considerable evidence that the Pacific coastal plain has been gradually desiccating over the past century. Perhaps it is a trend of much longer duration. In any event, within the memory of people still living, a number of families in San Juan Evangelista could supplement their incomes by fishing and collecting fresh water shrimp from the rivers and lagoons of the *municipio*, most of which have today disappeared entirely or are so sporadic and seasonal that they no longer support edible marine life.

For a long time irrigation has been very important to Isthmus Zapotecs. Small-scale river valley irrigation was almost certainly practiced in pre-Conquest times, although the earliest documentation known to me occurs in 1580 (Torres de Laguna). Almost as important as irrigation have been the seasonal inundations of rather extensive areas of the coastal plain during the rainy season when rivers and streams pour thousands of acre-feet of water out onto the plain from the vast watershed of a mountainous hinterland. While crop damage and flooding of dwelling sites have been frequent results, the silts carried by the flood waters have also provided a natural source of fertilizer, rendering many fields perpetually productive. A government irrigation and flood-control project which began operation in 1964 will eventually make year-round irrigation available to much heretofore unproductive land, but it also limits the possibility of seasonal inundations. One result might be the necessity of applying expensive commercial fertilizers on some fields to maintain fertility.

The two most prominent features of the Isthmus landscape are the mountains and the coastal plain. The Pacific plain, perhaps 20 miles in breadth at its widest point, is stalked by majestic segments of the imposing mountain chains which parallel the Pacific Ocean the length of two continents. Somewhat less formidable here than farther south, the mountains are nonetheless impressive as they rise abruptly behind the plain. Isthmus Zapotecs are plains-dwelling people. They avoid the mountain hinterland so much a part of their landscape as a dread and dangerous place. Stories circulate of carnivorous creatures, some mythical and perhaps some real, inhabiting the mountains, lying in wait for human prey. The hinterlands immediately surrounding the *Istmo* are not uninhabited by people, however. Since before the Conquest various ethnic groups, including Mixe, Zoque, Chontal, and others, have occupied the area, trading mountain products for Zapotec and Huave products of the sea and plain. These people, known collectively as *serranos*, are familiar to the plains-dwellers and some Isthmus Zapotecs have migrated to the mountain communities to raise coffee, displacing the older population almost entirely in a few cases, thus themselves becoming serranos to the remaining plains-dwellers.

On the coastal plain, too, other linguistic and ethnic groups have been present although Zapotecs have always been the major population of the area in historical times. One of these ethnic groups, the Huaves, who speak a language as distinct from Zapotec as African Bantu is from English, may have occupied the area when

Side street in late afternoon.

the first Zapotecs arrived from the north, perhaps about 1000 A.D., perhaps earlier. Today the small Huave population lives in several settlements on the sandspits of the Pacific Ocean. Probably their total population is no more than 5,000. By comparison, approximately 57,000 Zapotec speakers are listed in the 1960 Censo General, of a total Isthmus population of approximately 97,500.[1] By municipio, the percentages of Zapotec speakers vary from only 13 percent in the municipio of Salina Cruz to 96 percent in that of San Juan Evangelista, the average being approximately 60 percent. Somewhat more than half of all Zapotec speakers also speak Spanish, a figure which can be expected to continue to rise as school attendance increases. The Isthmus also contains a sizable population of persons who speak only the national language. This group, approximately 40 percent of the total population, reflects two ongoing processes with a long history in the Isthmus, immigration of non-Zapotecs into the area and acculturation of Zapotecs into the national culture through formal educational process and exposure to outside influences. Since language is the main criterion of ethnicity, Zapotecs who learn

---

[1] The figures are approximate because the census figures are compiled on the basis of *ex-distritos*. The two ex-distritos of the Isthmus include forty-four municipios, all but eleven of which are outside the traditional Isthmus Zapotec area. The figure of 57,000 for Zapotec speakers is probably much too low since Zapotec is the low-status language compared to the national language, Spanish. In any case, the percentage of the population which is biologically Zapotec would probably surpass 90 percent in the eleven Zapotec municipios were one to employ genetic rather than linguistic criteria.

only Spanish as children are classified as non-Zapotec in the government census even though they may be Zapotecs genetically.

Not only ethnically, but culturally and socially as well, the Isthmus of Tehuantepec is a mosaic of complex patterns. Some peoples speaking totally unrelated languages have quite similar cultures and life styles as, for example, Zapotec and Huave *campesinos*. Within the Zapotec-speaking population itself, on the other hand, one encounters a full range of social and cultural variation—from the poor illiterate campesino who speaks little or no Spanish to the wealthy, educated professional person (often a lawyer or an engineer) as urbane as any upper class citizen of the nation's capital. Basically, the Isthmus Zapotecs are still largely of the social type defined anthropologically as peasant and as such are in many ways comparable to peasant populations in other parts of the world. It is this majority peasant Zapotec population which forms the basis of the case study.

Many Isthmus Zapotecs retain a great deal of pride in their cultural heritage. Some Zapotec elites, both in the Isthmus and in the capital, have tried to encourage retention of the native language and ethnicity. Some of these individuals compose songs and poetry in Zapotec, often publishing them at their own expense, while others take pride in recording for posterity certain of *las costumbres* which are gradually disappearing from people's lives and memories. Popular songs in Zapotec are composed by local musicians also and are introduced to the public at fiestas. Some of these have become very popular regional songs. In these ways, Isthmus Zapotecs seem to be unique among Latin American indigenous populations. To my knowledge, no other ethnic or linguistic group in Mesoamerica currently produces literature and music in the native language.

2 / Binii gula'sa':
prehistory and history

PREHISTORY

Binii gula'sa' are the ancient ones, familiar to every Isthmus Zapotec through the frequent chance finds of ancient cultural materials. Informants report discoveries from time to time of urn burials, tripod pottery, very large *ollas*, and small stone figurines. Habitation sites are numerous but difficult to date from surface material which includes small obsidian points and tripod shards in the form of serpent heads very similar to those from Yagul, Valley of Oaxaca. A large carved stone lintel, also with serpent head motif, lies half buried in debris beside the oldest church in San Juan Evangelista. Few people are aware of its presence and none knows its origin. A few months after I left the field in 1967, a man excavating for a house foundation on a hilltop uncovered what was reported to be part of a *templo*. All of these things were left by the binii gula'sa', say the people, and the binii gula'sa' are the ancestors of the Isthmus Zapotecs, they believe. But that is a question even archaeologists cannot answer, for a great many different peoples have inhabited or passed through the Isthmian corridor for thousands of years, peoples whose languages cannot be determined from the archaeological record. The Pacific coastal plain must have served as a funnel for foot travelers between North and South America from the first, as people found the Gulf coast with its immense meandering rivers, swamplands, and dense tropical growth impassable.

Several habitation sites on the coastal plain excavated by Delgado (1961) revealed pre-Classic cultigens of maize, squash, and cotton as well as the remains of wild boar, badger, deer, turtle, shrimp, and a variety of birds and fish.

By glottochronology, Isthmus Zapotec language separated from the mother tongue about seven centuries ago, a date supported by recent archaeology at Mitla and Yagul, Valley of Oaxaca.[1] Since modern Isthmus Zapotec is also more closely related to the Mitla dialect of Valley Zapotec than to others, it is reasonable to postulate the Mitla-Yagul area as the point of origin. Perhaps the Huaves occupied

[1] Glottochronology is a method, developed by Morris Swadesh, whereby elapsed centuries since the separation of two or more related languages can be estimated through statistical analysis of cognates. The method assumes a similar rate of change for all languages and a constant rate within a single language which has led to criticism. However, archaeology and other dating methods often, as in the case of Zapotec, lend strong support to its reliability.

the coastal plain when the Zapotecs first entered the Isthmus, and were gradually displaced to their present marginal position at the edge of the Pacific by an expanding Zapotec population, a postulate still unverified.

Situated on a mountain high above the Tehuantepec River is the only well-known and impressive archaeological site of the Isthmus, Guiengola. For many years it was thought to have been constructed in the fourteenth century as a fortification against the Mexicas,[2] but archaeological investigations have revealed occupation of the site intermittently by various peoples, beginning in the Archaic Period (7000–3500 B.C.). Later levels contained Zapotec ceramics and Mayan figurines which Forster dated as contemporary with Monte Alban III (Forster 1953).

HISTORY

In 1496, Zapotec-Mixtec forces defended the Isthmus against Mexica attackers from the venerable Guinegola in a siege which lasted seven months. Finally, according to tradition, the Mexica gave up in defeat. Some of the Mixtec allies decided to remain in the Isthmus, founding the settlement of Mixtequilla which still exists at the foot of the mountain (Iturribarria 1960).

When the Spaniards arrived in 1523, El Centro was already a sizable settlement. The region was governed by Cosijopii, son of the Zapotec ruler of Zaachila, Valley of Oaxaca. Despite the reported defeat of the Mexica in 1496, the Spaniards found the Isthmus as well as the Valley and Sierra Zapotecs tributary to the Mexica (Gay 1950).

Cortes lost little time in turning his attention southward, once he was established in the Valley of Mexico. Alvarado passed through the Isthmus on his march to Guatemala in 1523, renaming the largest settlement Villa de Guadalcazar, a name which endured through the colonial period (Cajigas 1954). In 1526 Cortes himself journeyed to the Isthmus, hoping to find a natural waterway from Pacific to Atlantic. His plan was to explore along the Pacific coast, search for the waterway, and perhaps even send an expedition across the Pacific. He came prepared, with men and equipment to build and outfit seaworthy ships! Two ships were constructed eventually and floated on the great lagoon at San Mateo del Mar, only to be wrecked by el norte before they could put to sea. Later attempts proved more successful. In 1529 Diego de Ocampo sailed from the Isthmus to Peru, and other ships built here eventually sailed as far as the Molucas in the Pacific and to Baja California.

The Isthmus Zapotecs apparently offered no immediate resistance to the Spaniards. Cosijopii allowed himself to be converted to Christianity during Cortes' visit and was baptized Don Juan Cortes. At the time of his conversion, Don Juan held an estate befitting a king which included, among other amenities, a sylvan retreat at the foot of the mountains consisting of extensive gardens and a residence built around a natural pool formed by a great bubbling spring. Don Juan mag-

---

[2] Mexicas are popularly referred to as "Aztecs."

nanimously demonstrated his zeal and loyalty to the new religion by donating most of his considerable estate to the Church, but could not bring himself to part with his retreat. That remained in the royal family until his daughter, in a similar burst of Christian generosity, donated the last remnants of the regal estate to the padres after her father's death.

In 1528, Cortes received from the Spanish crown the title of Marques del Valle de Oaxaca along with a vast grant of land which included the greater part of what is today the state of Oaxaca. The immediate post-Contact years were marked by a decimation of indigenous populations of the Isthmus as dramatic as that reported for other regions of Mesoamerica. A population of 20,000 in 1550 declined in thirty years to 3,200, according to Torres de Laguna (1580). Certainly the thirty years before 1550 were no less critical. Then slowly after 1580 the population decline was halted and the trend gradually began to reverse itself. Some population experts believe that recovery to pre-Conquest levels was not reached until the present century, 400 years after the first wave of devastating European diseases swept over the New World.

San Juan Evangelista was almost surely a community before the Conquest. When it first appears in historical documents in 1543, it is a *barrio* of El Centro and that may well have been true from its beginning. In the year mentioned, the Dominican friars were constructing the cathedral and convent in El Centro. Don Juan Cortes "ordered the barrio of [San Juan Evangelista] which was made up of fishermen, to bring to the Dominicans and workers daily sufficient fish to feed eight people and their servants," reports Burgoa (Gay 1950). Today it is no longer possible for residents to earn a livelihood by fishing, but that change is so recent that some people still remember the dugout canoes, the breechclouts, and the type of nets used by fishermen when they were children.

Independence and Revolution, the Macrovista

No other specific mention of San Juan Evangelista is known until the mid-nineteenth century when it reenters the pages of history as a *pueblo rebelde*, an epithet which lingers still, to be thrown out in anger on occasion.[3] But there are recorded incidents during the intervening three centuries in the Isthmus as elsewhere of uprisings and insurrections among peoples dominated by the Spanish crown. *Juanecos* did not become rebeldes overnight, nor were they alone in their fight against what they perceived as oppression.

Around 1850, however, the political situation in the Isthmus was such that the people of the barrio of San Juan found themselves opposed to the leaders in El Centro who held the political power. The leaders, claimed opponents in San Juan, were outsiders (and indeed they probably were) interested only in exploitation of the Zapotec population. Although most of the dozen or more barrios of El Centro were as Zapotec as San Juan, only the Juanecos found the courage to resist decisions originating in El Centro. Perhaps their location behind the

---

[3] It is probable that local government documents and records would yield additional information for the existing lacuna between 1540 and 1850 with reference to San Juan Evangelista. Unfortunately, these sources were not available to the author.

mountain made control by El Centro officials more difficult than was true for the more vulnerable central barrios. In any case, between 1846 and 1868 San Juan repeatedly allied itself with San Jacinto, some 30 kilometers distant, to oppose El Centro political control. It was a time of great political turmoil on a national level and local issues were often national issues. At least once Juanecos were able to establish themselves briefly in the *palacio* of El Centro, and at least once San Juan was sacked and burned by their opponents, the people forced to flee into the countryside or seek refuge with their San Jacinto allies.

The climax came in 1867 when San Juan and San Jacinto allied themselves with Loyalist Porfirio Diaz to resist the French Intervention while El Centro joined the pro-French Imperialists (Cajigas 1954). At last the Juanecos were on the winning side.

During Diaz' long regime, 1876–1910, the Isthmus of Tehuantepec apparently enjoyed comparative peace and prosperity, the latter reaching a peak with the opening of the port of Salina Cruz in 1894 and the completion of the trans-Isthmus railroad in 1907. With the railroad came instant fame and fortune, locally called the *Epoca de Oro*, because the Isthmus of Tehuantepec was the shortest trade route between the Atlantic and the Pacific oceans. As many as fifty trains traversed the Isthmus daily bearing international cargoes, and there was a great influx of all types of persons hoping to capitalize on the boom. But, alas, it was all too brief. Only seven years later, the Panama Canal opened and the Golden Era of the Isthmus of Tehuantepec died as suddenly as it was born (Cajigas 1954).

There are many historical accounts of the stormy mid-1800s and of the Mexican Revolution (1910–1920). The Zapotecs were heavily involved in these political upheavals. The Isthmus, one must remember, has always been politically and militarily strategic by its very geographical nature. The Zapotecs provided their share of generals, war heroes, martyrs, and traitors, and their homeland has been no less a battleground in the history of Mexico than have the more famous battlefields of the north.

Independence and Revolution, the Microvista

Zapotec historians recount history somewhat differently from national historians, and oral traditions of historical events often emphasize points overlooked or unknown on the national level. One point is clear: History lives for the Isthmus Zapotecs in a very vital and personalized way. Juanecos especially hold Porfirio Diaz close to their hearts. He is their great hero of Mexican Independence. After a century, illiterate campesinos can point out spots where Diaz and his men camped, and they take great pride in recounting Diaz' personal interest and affection for Juanecos. "He promised to do anything for his friends, the Juanecos, and he always kept his promise," they state, these men who did not learn history from books. To Juanecos, Diaz' greatest deed was granting the status of independent municipio to San Juan Evangelista for its efforts against the French. History probably records otherwise because Benito Juarez, a Zapotec from the Valley of Oaxaca, was head of the national government at that time, 1868.

Local historical tradition is interesting also in the strong role it records for Zapotec women who sometimes fought beside their men but more often are portrayed as heroines who smuggled messages and supplies through enemy lines and provided key information about enemy plans and movements. Actually such roles were not unique to women of the Zapotec region during those turbulent years, but women may well have played a stronger role in the Isthmus than in other regions. Regardless of the historical facts, what is interesting is the importance attached to women's roles in historical events by Isthmus Zapotecs themselves. Where historians on the national level neglected to mention women's heroic deeds or recorded the deed but not the name, Zapotecs personalize their history with the names and kinship relations of heroic women and men with equal fervor. Perhaps this is no more than history personalized, but it may be another manifestation of that elusive quality of relationships between the sexes which has led more than a century of casual observers to perpetuate the myth of an Isthmus Zapotec matriarchate.

3 / San Juan Evangelista today

RELATIONSHIP TO LARGER COMMUNITY

The pueblo of San Juan Evangelista is the focal point of this book, but like all human communities, it does not exist in isolation. San Juan has very close ties with the wider Isthmus Zapotec community and cannot be accurately described except in the wider context.

The two largest communities of the Isthmus Zapotecs, El Centro and San Jacinto, are approximately 30 kilometers apart and contain between 40 and 50 percent of the total regional population. There are a number of other smaller towns, several with populations well over 5,000. Few people live in dispersed homesteads in the rural areas, even though perhaps the majority of Zapotecs are campesinos. For centuries they have been town dwellers and that is the mode of life they prefer. However, it is a mistake to think of Isthmus towns and cities in terms of towns and cities of the United States. They are quite different, having few of the amenities we tend to associate with an urban environment. Isthmus Zapotecs, however, conceptualize their larger settlements as urban and take great pride in them.[1] Indeed, there are no other communities of comparable size within a 150-mile radius.

As previously stated, until a century ago San Juan Evangelista was a barrio of El Centro. The ties which bind the two separate political entities continue to be very strong, especially in terms of economics and subsistence. Yet some of the old political animosity remains, often finding new causes and occasionally breaking into its more virulent forms—ambushes, vendettas, and mob actions which require the presence of state militia to keep the peace. But for the most part peace prevails on the surface, although the people have long memories.[2]

[1] An informant who took her teacher training and lived for several years in Oaxaca de Juarez expressed great admiration for El Centro, inquiring if I had not been surprised to find such a great city when I first arrived. On the other hand, tourists and residents of Mexican metropolitan areas generally view the Isthmus centers as exceptionally rural and lacking in comforts, either scorning them as impossibly backward and isolated or valuing them for their provincial quaintness.

[2] Several years prior to my fieldwork, the president of El Centro was assassinated by members of a political faction whose purported leader was a native son of San Juan Evangelista, although he had not lived in the pueblo for years. Justice being swift in the Isthmus, he was arrested and almost immediately met with some sort of fatal accident. The residents of San Juan Evangelista were so incensed by the sordid affair that economic sanctions in the form of a beer boycott were imposed on a prominent member of the opposing faction, a distributor for a major brand of beer. In 1966, trucks bearing that brand name were still prohibited from making deliveries or even entering San Juan Evangelista.

The central barrios of El Centro constitute the "downtown" section. This is where the market places, city hall and other government offices, bank, post office, telegraph office, public telephones, movie theaters, drugstores, and a relatively small number of commercial establishments are located. As in all of Latin America, traditionally the commercial center is also the most prestigious place to live, the "high-rent" district not only for businesses but for residences as well. Virtually all of the *mestizo* and other non-Zapotec families, as well as most of the wealthier, more mestizized Zapotecs, live in the central part of El Centro. Around the inevitable central plaza, streets are paved, and local and long-distance buses and trucks roar around the plaza, exhaust pipes unhampered by mufflers, 24 hours a day.[3] In this small area around the central plaza all the exciting contacts with the outside world take place. Weary, overheated tourists detour the block off the Inter-American Highway to buy a cold drink or mail a letter, rest briefly, and then flit away down the highway, but not before at least one woman from San Jacinto has tried to sell them a "silk" hammock or a girl from San Juan Evangelista has pushed her *totopos* under their noses with such persistence that they purchased a few in self-defense. The quadrangle is also the nerve center of all of El Centro, San Juan Evangelista, and the surrounding hinterland. News and gossip radiates out from here to the barrios and San Juan in a surprisingly rapid and efficient manner, and local news trickles into the center and spreads outward along similar routes, carried by women going to and from market and employees returning from jobs.

The six or so outlying barrios of El Centro lack most of the "urban" character of the center and differ little from San Juan Evangelista. The streets are unsurfaced, on the perimeters usually unlighted; *agua potable* from the district purifying plant may be lacking entirely or available only at a communal outlet; electricity may be lacking in *solares* or consist of no more than a single bare bulb. The farther from the center, the less likelihood that a given household will have "modern" plumbing (locally defined as a flush toilet, water piped into a shower, and some sort of drainage system), although households on the hillsides rather close to the center also have mostly primitive sanitary facilities due to the cost of piping water uphill. A number of houses in the outlying barrios have dirt floors and some, especially around the perimeters, are no more than *chozas*, with reed walls sometimes chinked with mud, thatched roofs, and dirt floors. During dry season the flat, sandy river bottom often attracts large numbers of squatters from elsewhere who build shelters from reeds, paper cartons, and whatever else they can find. When water released from the dam fills the river banks during rainy season the squatters must seek other shelter or be washed away. The city fathers are ashamed of the squatter settlements, and attempts are made to force the people to move on from time to time, but others soon replace them.

On the whole, however, most Zapotec dwellings are of *material*, locally made but relatively costly, adobe for walls and tiles for roofing, and often include cement floors. A house of material is highly valued as a status symbol, as a sign of being

---

[3] Streets around the central plaza were paved about three years prior to fieldwork. Before that, they were cobblestone. But even the paved streets are frequently covered with several inches of mud washed down from the hillsides during rainstorms.

In the market place.

"civilized." Many families reside in chozas near their fields part of the time, and these small native structures seemed to me to be quite comfortable and well suited to the climate as well as cheap and easy to erect.

Inhabitants of some of the outlying barrios are more isolated from the central district than are Juanecos, having to walk the two or more miles to and from the center when they lack bus fare or during hours when buses do not run. Taxis are available for the affluent in the center but infrequent and difficult to snag in the outlying areas. There are few private telephones, almost all belonging to businesses or professionals.

Residents of the central district of El Centro consider themselves socially superior to persons in the outlying areas. Generally speaking they are apt to have a higher standard of living, better education and income, and often are "outsiders," but even a poor Zapotec widow who happens to live in the central area because three generations of her family have occupied her modest house will feel herself to be more civilized simply by the location of the dwelling. Mestizos and other outsiders who live in the center look down on the rest of the population as *sin cultura*. As a native of Mexico City, whose family owns a business in El Centro, explained:

> Most people here don't know how to live in a civilized way. That's why we call them "sin cultura." They don't know how to enjoy life, just throw their money

Girl from San Juan Evangelista arriving at El Centro with stack of totopos *to sell.*

away on beer-drinking and fiestas. A trip to Veracruz or Tuxtla to them would be a big adventure. Some people have quite a bit of wealth but they don't have culture and they are too ignorant to enjoy the wealth they have. They live in the old way, invest in gold jewelry, spend time and money giving and attending fiestas, probably live in a house with no floors or plumbing, throw their garbage into the center of the solar, and allow the pigs and chickens to run all over the solar. They live on *pozol* and tortillas with a little salt shrimp and dry cheese and think that's "la vida." And the chances are good that they can't even write their own name.

Thus traditional Zapotec peasant culture is scorned by the majority of local elites, although the latter would be mostly rather middle-class in more urban settings. The Juanecos bear the heaviest burden of this attitude because they are the largest concentration of the most traditional peasant population in the immediate vicinity.

From the central district no sign directs the visitor to San Juan and few strangers are aware that a pueblo of more than 6,000 people lies just behind the mountain not more than a twenty-minute walk from the center of one pueblo to the center of the other. The only clues to San Juan's existence are the signs on the rickety, lumbering *urbanos*—El Segundo, Santa Inez, San Juan, and the other outlying destinations including *el panteon*. The buses come in, fill up, and leave the central district continuously during daylight hours. The bus to San Juan runs at half-hour intervals and like all the others is laden with women and girls, mostly in native dress, going home with baskets, bundles, and net bags filled with daily purchases of foodstuffs, sometimes including a brace of live iguanas, bound and gagged, a hobbled hen, or a live turkey. Usually the driver and the fare collector are the only men aboard.[4] The urbano gets under way with effort, creaking and groaning over the rough and narrow streets as it works its way toward San Juan, a gigantic metal version of the *criollo* sows that root the same path. At what appears to be the end of the street on the river bluff, the bus makes a 90-degree turn up hill, squeezes through a narrow passage hewn through solid rock, and emerges into San Juan Evangelista.

SAN JUAN EVANGELISTA, THE PUEBLO

The church dominates the visitor's first impression of San Juan. Standing just inside the entrance to the pueblo, it faces the entrance passageway rather than the center of San Juan, giving an impression of having turned its back on the pueblo, a stance perhaps symbolic of a mutual indifference between the citizens and the official Church. Still, the church structure is more attractive and in better repair than any in El Centro, for while there is general distrust and suspicion of the clergy, there is also great respect for the saints and a considerable degree of

---

[4] For the most part, men who have business in outlying areas hire a taxi, while resident men are away from the pueblos during daylight hours, most often working in their fields. The campesino who happens to be in El Centro during daylight hours will probably choose to walk home, saving the 30-centavo ($3\frac{1}{2}$ = U.S. cent) fare and leaving more space on the bus for the women and their ever-present *bultos*. As a rule Zapotec men do not carry burdens.

religious activity and piety in day-to-day living. Juanecos practice their folk Catholicism rather independently as they have for generations, sometimes to the amazement and distress of visiting *padres*.[5]

Although the usual practice has been to hire a priest from El Centro when needed, in 1966 a few prominent citizens of San Juan had succeeded in securing a resident priest and two nuns who had begun a parochial school for boys in the church compound. The young priest was forced to leave after a few months because of ill health. The two women stayed on for a time, but even the little confidence they had gained in the people of San Juan eventually flickered and died, and they too left.[6]

About three blocks beyond the church lies the central *parque*, appropriately modest for a former barrio of El Centro, bordered on three sides by streets and on the fourth by the small public market place, the *plazita*, where a few local women are always to be found selling or waiting for customers. Facing the parque and the plazita is the municipal building which houses the jail, the upper two or three grades of the public elementary school, and a small library newly established, plus the offices of the municipio. A block away stands the modest and ancient church of San Bartolo Xadani, still in use but bearing the marks of its age. Long ago it marked the focal point of a barrio by the same name, but today no one in San Juan remembers barrio boundaries.

There is no business district as such in San Juan, a reflection of its past history as barrio and its continuing dependence on El Centro. Five or six general stores, usually located in the front part of the owner's dwelling, are scattered over the pueblo. There are several *nixtamal* mills, each serving its particular neighborhood, and a variety of workshops of tailors, sandal makers, carpenters, jewelers, seamstresses, and the like, as well as the inevitable rash of *cantinas* and *tienditas*, all operated from the proprietors' residences. San Juan has no post office, no telegraph office, no drugstore, and only one medical doctor, relying on El Centro to fulfill such needs.[7] In these ways San Juan is as dependent as any outlying barrio of El Centro. But in the minds of Juanecos there is one enormous difference between the status of San Juan and the barrios.

That difference is political independence, and the residents of San Juan Evangelista cherish it intensely. Repeatedly informants' comments included: "San Juan es un pueblo libre." And, contrary to fact, most people will argue that this is a special political status accorded to very few pueblos in the entire nation. This special status they owe to their hero, Porfirio Diaz.

The pueblo of San Juan Evangelista has a population of approximately 6,300. Perhaps another 1,000 persons live in the municipio in the several unincorporated rancheros and on a few isolated farmsteads. Some families have permanent dwellings

---

[5] This is a pattern typical of many Mesoamerican peasant communities.

[6] The two nuns were rather young and certainly unprepared for life in a rural peasant community. When a *borracho* stumbled to their door one night and begged for sexual favors, they were properly outraged but genuinely perplexed at such barbarous audacity.

[7] Efforts were being made in 1968 to secure a telegraph office in San Juan. In 1969 a public telephone was installed in one of the tiendas, only to be taken out a short time later while the building underwent major alterations. It has probably since been reconnected.

in San Juan Evangelista and another house, often a choza, near their fields with various members of the family alternating between the two as work and business dictate. A sample of 210 households reveals a median household size of 5.6 persons. There are more than 1,100 households in San Juan.

Isthmus Zapotecs favor virilocal residence (that is, the newlyweds live with the husband's family after marriage), but lineally extended families of the sample households were equally divided between virilocal and uxorilocal residence (couple resides with wife's parents after marriage). Other things being equal, the virilocal pattern is followed; but if the bride is an only daughter, the bride's parents are considerably more prosperous than the groom's, the groom is an orphan, or the virilocal household is crowded, the young couple may find living with the wife's parents more convenient. Today most young couples express a desire to establish their own household immediately upon marriage and a few manage to do so. Most find it economically impossible for a few years at least.

Most residents of San Juan were born in the pueblo and have never lived elsewhere. Only 5 of 119 household heads were not natives, and all but one of these were born in nearby municipios. As the population pyramid would indicate, a significant number of young men between the ages of fifteen and thirty-five are absent from the pueblo. They leave to seek better job opportunities elsewhere and to attend school. They return intermittently and keep in contact with their kin but the same forces which cause them to leave usually prevent their returning permanently to San Juan Evangelista. This emigration pattern, of long duration, has serious consequences not only for the marriageable girls left behind but also for the pueblo as a whole since the more ambitious, enterprising, and perhaps more intelligent young men of each generation who might otherwise have made the greatest contributions to their home community are forced by economic circumstances to leave. The other side of the emigration coin benefits the pueblo, for emigrant Zapotecs tend to remain emotionally attached to the place of their birth, maintaining extensive kin ties, and returning for public and family fiestas whenever possible. Often migrants send money to parents and siblings, and not infrequently children of siblings and even cousins live for years with their city kinfolk in order to benefit from the better educational opportunities in city schools. Favored migration destinations are Mexico City, Veracruz, and the cities on the Gulf coast of the geographical Isthmus, the latter attractive because of proximity and job opportunities in the petroleum industries. At least two "colonias'" of Mexico City are heavily populated with Isthmus Zapotecs.

Traditionally, Zapotec has been the first language of all Isthmus Zapotecs and one of the most important means of maintaining their ethnicity, but it has also been a deterrent to integration and opportunity in the national culture. Formerly children only learned the national language when they attended school and many children did not attend regularly enough to learn the language. Nowadays many parents recognize that the key to improving one's economic and social status in the national culture is a command of the national language. A few more progressive parents who speak fluent Spanish try to teach their children only Spanish. This is more apparent in other communities however. In San Juan Evangelista less than 4 percent of the population speaks only the national language, and 96 percent speaks Zapotec, 43 percent monolingually (VIII Censo General). In San Juan, with the highest incidence of retention of the indigenous language of any Zapotec community in the Isthmus, one seldom hears the national language except in schools, on official occasions, and when residents are speaking to outsiders. Even the announcements made over the public address system are usually in Zapotec. By contrast, more than 60 percent of the inhabitants of El Centro speak only Spanish. According to the 1960 census, 28 percent of the residents of San Juan age thirteen and over are literate, but if the test of literacy were comprehension of a first-grade reader instead of the word of the individual, 10 percent literacy might be a generous figure. Formal schooling is not stressed for girls, and this is reflected in literacy statistics which indicate that twice as many men as women are literate.

There are two primary schools in San Juan, one with six grades, the other with only the first three. Until 1967, the only secondary school (comparable to our junior high school) was in El Centro. Beginning in 1967, seventh-grade evening classes were being offered to about 40 young men in San Juan. Shockingly few children graduate from primary school and fewer still continue beyond that level. In 1967, 104 students were continuing their education beyond the sixth grade, less than 9 percent of San Juan's populations between the ages of fifteen and twenty-three! It is not always indifference to education that keeps children at home, although this is sometimes a factor. More often families cannot afford to send all their school-age children to classes simultaneously. Boys attend more than girls because education is perceived as more useful to boys and because girls are more useful at home. Although 46 percent of the boys and 31 percent of the girls between the ages of six and fourteen were enrolled in school in 1967, perhaps only about one third attended classes regularly. Often one or two children are sent to school for a year or so and then they remain at home while one or two others are sent, all ending with a minimal and equally ineffective education. Another method is to educate one son for a profession or white collar job, the whole household pouring resources toward that goal, making great sacrifices to insure the parents against a destitute old age and at the same time elevating the family's social status.

4 / The subsistence base

PATTERNS OF SUBSISTENCE, TRADITIONAL AND MODERN

At first European contact, Zapotecs were already accomplished cultivators, sharing with other Mesoamericans the long history of New World plant domestication. In the Isthmus people were growing corn, varieties of squash and chiles, cotton, and a wide variety of other vegetables and tropical fruits. One of the fruits, the zapote, was so prevalent in the entire Zapotec area that the Spaniards referred to the people by the name of the fruit.[1] Irrigation was essential in many places and was practiced wherever their paleotechnology made it possible. Isthmus Zapotecs were fortunate in the abundant supply of fish and shrimp readily available in the great saltwater lagoons, the sea, rivers, and freshwater lagoons. Sometime in the distant past the people discovered how to preserve these products by salting and drying in the sun. The Gulf of Tehuantepec, near the shores at least, has a high salt content. Perhaps centuries before the Conquest people built earthen salt pans at the edges of the saline lagoons which could be filled with salt water and then allowed to drain, leaving only the dry salt crystals. Salted fish and shrimps are still the main sources of whole protein in the native diet, and the salt pans of the coastal lagoons continue to be a major source of salt for the entire republic.

The Spaniards introduced many new cultigens, useful domestic animals, and a new technology based on beasts of burden which set in motion changes in subsistence techniques all over Mesoamerica. While many of the European cultigens were not suited to the Isthmus climate, chickens, burros, horses, cattle, sheep, goats, and oxen along with oxcarts and the primitive Mediterranean plow revolutionized agriculture. Although mechanization is presently being introduced, for the majority of Zapotec campesinos oxen, oxcarts, and Mediterranean plows are as essential today as they have been for the past four centuries.

Zapotecs practice mixed cash-subsistence farming, raising some crops totally for sale and others mostly for home consumption. Older informants in San Juan remember when sugar cane was the principal cash crop and quite a profitable one

[1] Zapotecs call themselves za, "the people," when they have occasion to refer to themselves as an ethnic group, which is rare. In practice they follow the widespread Mesoamerican custom of identifying themselves and others by the pueblo of birth and by region rather than by ethnic or linguistic criteria. A native of San Juan is a Juaneco, a native of the Isthmus is an Istmeño. Thus a resident of San Juan will be referred to regionally as a Juaneco and as an Istmeño when outside the region.

for a time in the early quarter of this century. Then prices fell on the international market to very low levels and canefields were gradually converted to other more profitable crops. The triad of bananas, mangoes, and coconut palms became popular in irrigated, wind-protected fields and continues to be important although not certainly very profitable. The pattern is to plant bananas in the plot and mangoes and coconuts around the perimeter. Mangoes, which become very large, dense trees, offer additional wind protection to the delicate banana plants while the tall, slender coconut palms can be planted between the mango trees, producing coconuts without taking additional space.

Recent introductions include sesame and sorghum, both totally cash crops, but the ancient maize remains the great crop favorite because of its versatility (cash or subsistence), its familiarity, and its vast importance in native diet. Government agronomists are encouraging the cultivation on a larger scale of some long established crops such as tomatoes, sweet potatoes, and native flowers in an effort to increase cash income sources.[2]

Land Tenure and the Social System

The social system is conceptualized as a great network of interrelationships and interdependencies. A shift in one part, perhaps a change so small it is unnoticed by the people themselves, may eventually engender unanticipated and important changes in other parts of the social system. One of the most obvious areas where changes begin is the subsistence base—crops, technology, and amount of arable land per family, for example. In agrarian social systems the total amount of land available, its distribution patterns, and the types of land tenure are so important to understanding the total social system that they are among the first subjects the fieldworker hopes to broach. In San Juan Evangelista, land is a very delicate subject. Direct questions by outsiders will be met with evasions, fabrications, or simply silence because Juanecos find themselves in an enviable but insecure position regarding the very core of their existence, land.

Basically there are two types of land tenure in the Isthmus: private and communal. Private property, most familiar to us, includes the right of the individual to sell the land. Communal property, on the other hand, does not include this right but only the right of the individual to use the land for a certain period of time. The title to the land remains with the community. San Juan Evangelista is unique among the Isthmus municipios in that its communal land dates from its separation from El Centro in 1868 at which time several thousand *hectares* of land were granted the new municipio. Other communal land tenure dates from the years after the Mexican Revolution (1910–1920) when the national government redistributed large holdings to groups of campesinos who formed *ejidos*. There is some

---

[2] Actually a great many common vegetables and fruits are not suited to the Isthmus climate. These include such staples as beans and onions and such familiar and mundane vegetables as white potatoes. All of these must be imported from higher elevation. Beans and onions are the only imports that are regular items in native diet. White potatoes are a luxury food. Even hybrid maize varieties have proved difficult to grow under local conditions. Although experimentations by government agronomists continue, most campesinos still plant the old inbred *criollo* maize.

ejidal land in the Isthmus, but private tenure is the more common type. Thus, San Juan is unique not only in its long history of communal tenure but also in the large amount of its total land area which remains in communal as opposed to private tenure (80 and 20 percent respectively).

In 1868 nobody worried much about precise municipio boundaries. Most of the land was marginal, supporting spinous scrub forest, and used mainly for gathering wild plant foods, a little hunting, firewood, and making charcoal. It would support some livestock during most of the year, but animals usually had to be fed supplementally toward the end of the long dry season. Certain parts of el monte could be farmed by slash-and-burn techniques in a pinch, but this method produced a poor crop for the amount of work involved and never was favored.[3] In spite of the poor quality of much of the land, the people of San Juan looked upon their communal lands as a vast untapped reservoir of resources. Many Zapotec campesinos in surrounding municipios had become alienated from the land over time by means fair and foul, and the message was not lost on the Juanecos. The municipio apparently undertook a program of land acquisition which appears to have continued until recently.

All this communal land made Juanecos feel especially fortunate compared to their neighbors but it also generated a high level of anxiety and suspicion, a suspicion which seems to border on paranoia at times. Municipio boundaries, never certain, have suddenly become more critical as population has increased and at the same time the possibility of reclamation of much of the land through extensive irrigation has recently become a reality. Anthropologists have postulated a close relationship between encysted or closed peasant communities and communal land tenure.[4] Although San Juan is not completely encysted, it is certainly the most conservative, self-protective municipio in the region by a number of criteria including retention rate of native language, anxiety and suspicion toward outsiders, and Juanecos' reputation in El Centro as *muy cerrados*. Almost certainly anxiety over land has increased since the initiation of the regional irrigation project. Juanecos have tried, more or less successfully, to keep government surveyors off their land; the municipio is embroiled in several lawsuits over boundaries; and open discussions of land with or before outsiders are discouraged.

Paradoxically, communal tenure has worked to pull the community together against the outside world, and at the same time it has worked to create internal dissension and factionalism. Some progressives feel that the municipio is "land poor." They urge that some of the land should be sold to neighboring municipios

---

[3] Slash-and-burn cultivation involves cutting, drying, and burning the native ground cover (here scrub trees and bushes) and planting the crop in the ashes. Where employed, the method usually entails opening new plots after a few seasons and abandoning the old ones as they become less productive, a system requiring a great deal of land.

[4] Wolf defines as closed peasant communities those which "restrict their membership, maintain a religious system, enforce mechanisms which ensure the redistribution or destruction of surplus wealth, and uphold barriers against the entry of goods and ideas produced outside the community" as opposed to the open peasant community "where communal jurisdiction over land is absent, membership is unrestricted, and wealth is not redistributed" (Wolf 1967:235). San Juan Evangelista is not a completely closed peasant community, yet it possesses in varying degree a number of the characteristics of a closed community.

who are creating problems about boundaries and the money used for desperately needed public improvements such as roads, land leveling, auxiliary canals, and other projects. The conservatives consider this a sell-out and from bitter past experience believe the money would disappear into politicians' pockets and result in little or no public good.

Communal tenure does not necessitate the working of land cooperatively. In San Juan, families are allotted individual plots of land which they then farm independently just as they do private property. The communal plots are to revert to the community after two years of nonuse or at the death of the original applicant, but probably neither of these rules has ever been enforced. Many households in San Juan still farm communal land which their parents or grandparents were allotted, often not aware that it is not private property until they try to sell it. Communal land can be converted to private property by paying a prescribed amount ($750 per hectare in 1967).[5] Such converted land cannot be sold by the original owner for more than the conversion price plus improvements. Heirs of the original owner may sell the land at market price. About 20 percent of San Juan's land is privately owned at the present time, including virtually all of the choice irrigated and wind-protected fields fanning out from the edge of the pueblo for an average of perhaps 3 miles. These *terrenos de labor* are favored for bananas, mangoes, coconuts, and other fruits, but a considerable number of plots are also planted to maize, and some devoted to sesame.

With an abundance of land and communal tenure, one might assume that every household would have some land but this is not the case. Sixteen percent of a small sample of forty-four households reported that they did not farm, either because there was no able-bodied man in the household or the men of the household had full-time occupations which left no time for farming, such as potters, carpenters, and schoolteachers. Farming, however, is the main occupation of the majority of men in San Juan Evangelista, and perhaps 90 percent of the households gain part of their income from agriculture.

Other Property and Ownership Rights

In addition to the fields held in private ownership, the most important items of property include *solares*, household equipment, animals, farm equipment, clothing, and jewelry. Sons normally inherit the solar of the parents while daughters are expected to move to the husband's solar at marriage. But daughters always have the right to return to their natal solar to live if they are widowed, and they have the right to remain in the solar all their lives if they do not marry, brothers supporting them if necessary. If there are two or more sons and the solar is large, it may be partitioned off as each son marries and eventually split into several small solares. Fields, when privately owned, are inherited bilaterally, although sons seem to inherit the best and largest fields. All tools, oxcarts, and other farming implements belong to men as do the large domestic animals. Oxen, tools, and equipment are usually

---

[5] All monetary values are given in Mexican pesos throughout the monograph unless otherwise stated. At the time of fieldwork, 1966–1967, the rate of exchange was approximately 12.5 pesos to one U.S. dollar.

inherited by sons, but herds of cattle and goats are divided more or less equally among all the children. Household furnishings are simple and few and invariably are considered a part of the solar when an estate is settled. The daughters have already received dowries at marriage consisting of a *baul* containing clothing and a variable amount of gold coin jewelry, depending on the family's resources. The jewelry belongs to the wife and is normally inherited by daughters, although no heirloom value is attached to it. Because jewelry functions primarily as a form of investment and collateral, it is rare for the same pieces to be passed on from mother to daughters through more than one generation, rare even for a mother still to possess the jewelry from her dowry when her daughters marry. Jewelry is owned by women, but it is pawned or sold for the benefit of the household just as land is, although much more frequently. The order of preference for raising cash to meet an emergency is generally: selling pigs, selling cattle other than oxen, pawning jewelry, selling jewelry, selling oxen, pawning land, and selling land. Since many households do not own cattle and some do not own pigs, pawning jewelry is the most frequent first choice, with jewelry selling close behind. Pawned or sold jewelry will be retrieved or replaced as soon as finances permit. There is a great deal of trade and pawning of gold jewelry, much of which is carried on by women, but most of the large money-lending operations are run by men. The government pawnshop in El Centro, which averages 800 transactions per month, represents a very small part of the total volume of transactions because most persons prefer the more liberal terms and higher interest rates of the private lenders.

Except for earrings and an occasional modest necklace, women wear gold jewelry only at fiestas where the more prosperous may literally be laden with heavy coin collars and necklaces, elaborate earrings, and perhaps two or three rings on each finger of both hands. But one does not have to be wealthy to wear embroidered *trajes* and gold jewelry to fiestas. Both can be borrowed or rented for a nominal fee, although that is usually only the resort of visiting outsiders and an occasional wily maiden hoping to snare a *novio*.

Men, with some exceptions to be discussed later, do not wear jewelry, but a man without sisters may inherit it, and if the man is going to pawn jewelry for masculine purposes such as buying seed corn, either he or the wife may carry the jewelry to a money-lender.

Sexual Division of Labor

All human societies observe certain rules when it comes to what tasks are considered appropriate for each sex, although the rules vary from one society to the next. Division of labor by sex seems to be an efficient way to carry out everyday functions of households even in industrialized societies such as our own where the household is mainly a consuming unit. In peasant and tribal societies where the household may be both the production and consumption unit, the division of labor by sex is generally rather strictly prescribed.

In San Juan the household is the basic production unit as well as the basic consumption unit. Paleotechnic farming, while it is the main occupation of the majority of male household heads, is not a lucrative venture under the best of conditions because of its high labor requirements and low productivity. As a result, households diversify. The more occupations and skills members of a household command, the more secure is the household against economic disaster. All productive members of the household are expected to have one or more means of bringing money into the household. Very often an individual learns several skills which he practices part-time in addition to his regular occupation. A man who considers his major occupation farming (which includes the care of

A wealthy matron displays her gold alhajas.

large animals such as oxen, cattle, horses, and goats) may also be a barber in the evenings and perhaps make fireworks in his spare time.

Most wives state that their principal occupation is "housewife," a term which includes a variety of economic functions not normally included in the term in English. For example, virtually every adult woman in San Juan can prepare tor-

Girl dressed in her first traje Tehuana *embroidered by the wearer with the help of her aunt.*

tillas and some other food for sale if the need arises. It is a rare household that does not include at least one woman who regularly processes and sells something. The vast majority of women do so intermittently at least, but even if selling is a regular activity it is almost never considered an occupation.

The list of women's occupations in Table 4-1 is the author's construct in that women *always* gave homemaking as their principal occupation, their income-producing activities being considered a normal part of homemaking. Principal occupations were elicited by rephrasing the question along lines of what they usually did to produce income and how much time they spent at such activities. From a comparison of men's and women's principal occupations, several things are apparent. First, no women are employed for wages, jobs which are rare and highly prized because any type of regular income, no matter how little, is thought to be economically advantageous compared to self-employment. Women normally

TABLE 4–1   PRINCIPAL OCCUPATIONS OF SAMPLE HOUSEHOLD HEADS BY SEX

Men (N 194)		*Women (N 174)*	
Occupation	*Numbers*	*Occupation*	*Numbers*
Agriculture		*Producer-Vendor*	
Campesino	115	Tortillera-Totopera	68
Day Laborer	1	Baker	9
Dairyman	1	Seamstress	7
Crafts		Prepared Foods	10
Tailor	8	*Revendor*	
Jeweler	7	Tiendita Operator	11
Musician	6	Revendors in Market Place	10
Carpenter	6	Traveling Revendors	7
Potter	5	Comerciante	4
Mason	4	Cantina Operator	2
Barber	3	*Other*	
Butcher	3	Housewife	41
Shoemaker	2	School Teacher	1
Brick Maker	1	Practical Nurse	1
Baker	1	Masseuse	1
Radio Repairman	1		
Oxcart Repairman	1		
Employees			
Clerical Worker	8		
School Teacher	3		
Wage Worker	2		
Truck Driver	1		
Soldier	1		
Mechanic	1		
Tradesmen			
Comerciante	7		
Traveling Revendor*	1		
Cantina Operator	1		
Other			
Masseur	1		

*Native of Oaxaca de Juarez.

Men bringing home firewood from el monte.

do not acquire the skills for wage and salary work. If they do, as in the case of the schoolteacher, they may not find a position because competition from men will be keen. Second, of twenty-six male occupations and fourteen female occupations, only eight are filled by both sexes. Of these, seamstress-tailor and masseur-masseuse are sex-specific (tailors make men's clothing, seamstresses make women's clothing), and the four women *comerciantes* and the one male traveling revendor all represent half of husband-wife teams. The only listed occupations considered equally suitable for either sex are baker and potter. But even in pottery making women usually specialize in small items, and men in large, heavy ones. Third, a difference which is not apparent in Table 4-1 relates to time spent practicing a principal occupation. Relatively few women devote what would be considered full-time by male standards to their principal occupation. This is not surprising since women's income-producing principal occupations compete with a number of other household duties, many of which take precedence over producing income.

Processing and Selling

The traditional and still prevalent basic division of labor between the sexes in San Juan Evangelista is simply this: Men are the producers and women are the processors and vendors of the men's production. This basic theme is expanded and adjusted to meet the individual needs of the particular household. The processing-vending role of women is extremely important to the economic success of the household, equally as important as the producer role of the men, as will become apparent. The most common processing-vending operation (and probably one of the least profitable because of competition and market limitations) is making tortillas and totopos for sale from maize produced by the household. Every adult

End of a hard day's work.

woman possesses the necessary skills and most make tortillas for their own household at least part of the time.[6] Since it is a time-consuming job, the woman may prefer to buy tortillas from a neighbor daily or occasionally. The middle-class mestizo population of El Centro offers another outlet because tortillas are usually not made at home unless there are servants to do it.

If a Juaneca makes tortillas all day, which she rarely does, she can earn from $8 to $10, which compares favorably with what a man can earn by working for wages in the fields. Both jobs are of equally low prestige because neither is thought to require any special skills and neither produces enough income for the daily needs of even the smallest household. More often a young woman tied to her household by small children earns a few extra *pesos* by making only enough extra tortillas for a neighbor or two.

The making of totopos is more involved, requiring an oven which all households do not have, at least $3 of scarce firewood, and the undivided attention of the *totopera* from start to finish. Thus, making totopos takes on some of the aspects of a specialization. Since it is a day-long job (once the oven is heated the totopos must be baked three or four at a time without pause) and one not amenable to interruptions, it is often taught to teen-age daughters. Because of

---

[6] Sixty-eight percent of the sample households made tortillas for their own household use almost daily.

the keeping qualities of totopos, which tortillas lack, there is always a ready market. Many are exported to other parts of the republic. With the same amount of *nixtamal* as required for tortillas, a woman can net between $10 and $16 per day making totopos. It is a dreaded task, however, because the totopera must lean over the open barrel-shaped oven and place her entire lower arm inside to paste the raw totopo on the oven wall, repeating the motion to remove it after baking. Thus she must stand over the hot oven for hours, inserting her bare arm every minute or two. Women who regularly make totopos are said to bear the marks of their occupation in badly scarred hands and arms from the inevitable burns. It is rumored that if one pursues the occupation too many years she will lose her eyesight from the toxic effects of heat and smoke. Often the young totopera is persuaded to keep at her task only because she is allowed to take the totopos to sell on the streets of El Centro in the late afternoon, a reward as valued by San Juan girls as allowing a sixteen-year-old to take the family car in our culture.

There are numerous types of processing and selling, many of them requiring the purchasing of some or all of the raw materials. Some common activities are: selling sliced cucumbers, pineapple, oranges and other "snack" foods to passersby in front of one's house; buying fish and shrimp from coastal people, salting and drying them in one's solar, and selling them locally or in urban markets; buying sugar and *cacao* beans and preparing chocolate tablets for sale; buying sea turtle eggs in season, boiling and selling them immediately or drying them to sell later; making *refrescos* of crushed fruit, water, and sugar and selling the beverage by the glass to passersby; and preparing a great variety of cooked foods for sale in the market places or on the streets.

There are also a great many things which can simply be bought in bulk and sold in very small quantities at higher prices because most households operate on a minimal cash basis, buying only enough of an item for immediate needs.[7] Some households also produce a number of things which can be sold without processing— for example, bananas, mangoes, and maize. A prestigious business venture, but one which seems to earn little if anything, is the *tiendita*, often no more than a shelf just inside the house entrance stocked with a few staple items for sale. Common items include such durables as soap, brooms, matches, beans, cigarettes, and candles. If the tiendita is near one of the schools perhaps a few inexpensive notebooks and pencils, hard candy, and chewing gum will comprise the inventory. Whether or not one actually nets any income, there are advantages in having a tiendita in one's house. The family can draw on its stock, which is purchased "wholesale," and the mere fact of the tiendita's presence adds to the family's social status. Although the possibility seems never to be realized, people believe that the tiendita may lead them into becoming a big comerciante some day.[8] The husband, brother, or son may provide the initial small capital outlay to begin a tiendita, but

---

[7] This is due in part to the lack of means of preserving perishable foods in a tropical climate, but it also applies to such staples as soap powder, sugar, rice, and beans. For example, a woman preparing to wash clothes buys just enough soap to do the amount of laundry at hand. Part of this is due to economic necessity and part of it is simply habit.

[8] Of the four or five more successful comerciantes in San Juan Evangelista, none began with a tiendita.

wives, mothers, grandmothers, or maiden aunts invariably operate them. How many tienditas are in operation at any one time is difficult to determine. They come in to existence and disappear as Arabian sheiks fold their tents and steal away in the night. Perhaps about 10 percent of the total households operate stores ranging in size from the smallest tiendita to the largest commercial enterprise in the pueblo, with most falling in the small range.

The admired comerciante is a man engaged in several different business enterprises of which the comparatively large, well-stocked tienda is usually one. While his wife tends the store, perhaps he also runs a *cantina*, owns or rents several farms operated with hired labor, almost surely lends money on land and jewelry, and probably acts as a buyer of local crops (maize, mangoes, bananas, and such) either on commission for a city wholesaler or on his own. Although the entire household is involved, often including one or more married sons and their wives, the elder male household head is the comerciante.

Selling by Men

As stated earlier, basically men produce and women process and sell, but there are certain exceptions. When maize is sold unshelled directly after harvest, the man usually seeks a buyer, perhaps a local comerciante, and delivers the maize to him by the *carreta*. The same is true of mangoes if they must be sold locally to a wholesaler, and men also sell the large animals, whose care and maintenance is also their responsibility. Craftsmen often sell their own products, either from the shop or by delivering them to customers, but some men (for example, potters) concentrate on their craft and let their wives handle the selling. Comparing men's and women's selling, one finds a clear difference in quantities, types of sales, and context of negotiations. Men sell large quantities of those products which can be sold immediately after harvest; sales are usually made by men to a wholesaler (except in the case of animals); and the context of the sales negotiations will not be the market place. Women sell in essentially three contexts: the home, the streets, and the market places. Men sometimes conclude a sale agreement in the home but never sell in the streets or in the market places.[9]

Selling by Women

The market places are overwhelmingly a woman's milieu. In addition to more than 350 permanent vendors who pay a fee to the *ayuntamiento* for their space, there are anywhere from 200 to perhaps 1,000 *ambulantes* per day, women who have no permanent space but squat or stand in the aisles or move around through the market places and adjacent streets selling their wares. Most of these women sell products of their household, and the quantities sold in any one day are usually quite small. One area of one of the market places is designated as a wholesale area.

---

[9] Approximately 10 percent of the more than 350 permanent vendors in the El Centro market places are men, almost all non-Zapotecs. Two or three Zapotec men have become owners of *puestos* rather by accident than design. In one case, an adult son who had helped his mother since childhood, gradually took over the entire operation until his mother more or less retired. In another case, the man had been hired as an orphan boy to help in the puesto of a mestizo. He inherited the business when the old man died.

Carrying a watermelon home from market.

Here women will sell local products either by the *cesto* or in lots as small as a half dozen items, the larger the purchase the lower the price. Truckloads of imported fruits such as oranges and pineapples are sold in this same type of graduated wholesale-retail price structure which allows many Zapotec revendors to buy a dozen or two fruits, and make a few pesos by reselling them by the slice.[10] A woman may sell every day for a week or so seasonally, once or twice a week as when she has enough ripe bananas to make the effort worthwhile, or a couple of hours a day at a particular time, as when she sells tortillas or prepared foods. The pattern of her market selling will be conditioned by the products she sells.

In the market places the cusomers too are almost all women. The market places, in fact, are the supermarkets of the Isthmus, the only place fresh fruits and vegetables, fresh meat, fish, and poultry can be purchased and the most convenient place to purchase all sorts of staples, notions, hardware, clothing, and yard goods, as well as a wide variety of prepared foods to eat on the spot or carry out. The several small grocery stores outside the market place in El Centro sell *ultramarinos* almost exclusively. Their customers are mainly local elites and tourists, the only people who can afford such luxuries. Thus, the entire population depends on the market places for their daily food needs.

During the two or three rush hours (7 to 10 A.M.) the aisles of the market places are jammed with housewives or their servants purchasing the daily food supply for the household.[11] A popular vendor may make 30 or more sales per hour during the busy period and total as many as 150 sales per day. Sales dwindle after 11 A.M. and by 2 P.M. the market stalls are deserted. About 4 P.M. vendors begin arriving to sell to the supper trade, taking up posts on the street outside the market place where it is cooler. These women are mostly different individuals from the morning vendors. Items for breakfast the following day are also sold at this time. By 8 P.M. this group of vendors has dispersed for the night, but meantime, beginning about 6 P.M., other women have set up portable tables and benches around the central plaza, where they serve meals prepared at home and on their portable charcoal burners. These portable restaurants are in operation until about 10 P.M. on ordinary nights but remain open until 2 or 3 A.M. when there are social events such as fiestas and dances which might bring late customers.

So far we have described only selling in El Centro. There are also several small plazitas in outlying sections such as the one in San Juan where Juanecas, from ten to thirty at any one time, sell to other Juanecas a small selection of prepared dishes, tortillas, sweet rolls, cheese, tomatoes, onions, and fresh beef. Compared to the central market places (the supermarket), the plazitas are the corner grocery where one goes for last minute or emergency food purchases. Their popularity is greatest between 6 and 8 A.M. when many housewives send children to make purchases for breakfast.

But Juanecas often go farther afield to sell. Some San Juan products such as bananas, mangoes, coconuts, and coconut tree seedlings, plus small quantities of

---

[10] Most of this type of revending takes place in front of or near the revendor's home in outlying areas and is often the task of young girls. Some girls from El Centro sell around the central plaza, however.

[11] See footnote 7.

Scene in outdoor market place.

many other local fruits, are regularly taken to San Jacinto, the regional trade center, where prices are apt to be higher and sales more brisk than in El Centro.[12] Selling in San Jacinto requires the entire day plus the time and expense involved in the 30-mile bus trip. Usually it is well after dusk when the women, from six to thirty depending on the season, return from San Jacinto, wearily trudging into San Juan with several empty baskets carried one in the other atop their heads, dirty and exhausted from squatting in the tropical sun all day at the edge of the dusty San Jacinto streets.[13]

A few women are *viajeras*, traveling more or less constantly, perhaps between the coastal villages and Oaxaca de Juarez, buying and selling on both ends of the circuit. Women whose households raise mangoes often take these fruits to Oaxaca de Juarez periodically during the two-month mango season, at least doubling their

[12] Prices are higher in San Jacinto because many of San Juan Evangelista products are difficult to grow around the drier, windier San Jacinto area. Sales are more brisk because this is the main regional trade center, drawing customers from a wide area of the mountains and coast.

[13] San Jacinto practices a type of local protectionism by reserving all shaded places for local vendors. Outsiders, including of course Juanecas, are assigned space at the edge of the streets outside the market structure where they are forbidden to erect shades. The place where Juanecas sell is in full sun until about 2 p.m. on the average.

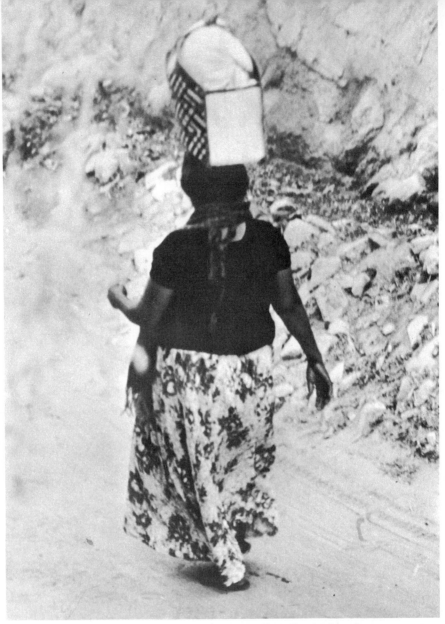

Woman carrying basket of food to sell in the market place.

net profit compared to selling them locally on a glutted market. This is wholesale selling in large quantities but it is always done by women. Once the fruits are harvested and delivered to the solar (and harvesting of fruits often involves the whole family), they become the wife's responsibility. She must hire local transport to El Centro and then find and bargain with a *fletero* to haul them to Oaxaca.[14] A woman may have twelve or more cestos of mangoes, each weighing about 200 pounds, in a single shipment. Once shipment is arranged by truck, the Juaneca

[14] During mango season it may take a woman two or three days to locate a fletero with space for her cargo since there is a great demand for fleteros at this time.

Woman going home from market place.

travels by second-class bus in order to arrive in the city ahead of the mangoes. The fletero will deliver the mangoes to a particular street where mangoes are sold wholesale. Most of the vendors at this time of year will also be women from the Isthmus since this is mango season there but not elsewhere. Several vendors will probably be from San Juan. Depending on the number of cestos she has, the Juaneca may sell all the mangoes the first day and return home on the night bus, or she may have to stay over two or even three days, in which case she pays a peso for a sleeping space in the patio of a private residence on the same street. It is a rare Juaneca who ventures out of the immediate vicinity of the market place when she sells in Oaxaca. More often she does not leave the particular street where her product is sold. For example, one informant, Lucia, had been bringing mangoes to the Oaxaca market for the past six or seven seasons, making from six to eight trips each season. A woman of exceptional intelligence and curiosity about the world, she visited the central part of the city for the first time with me, although it is only a distance of about three blocks from the street where she sells.

The reasons women confine themselves to the Oaxaca market place are many. Primarily, the object of the trip is to sell the mangoes and return home as rapidly as possible in order to arrange shipment for the successive picking. Second, the vendor cannot leave her mangoes unattended except for brief periods when a neighbor will sell for her. And further, there is really very little incentive to leave the market area since everything a woman may wish to buy is available in the market place and at lower prices than elsewhere in the city. Lucia had always wanted to see the cathedral but feared she would lose her way, being unable to read the street signs and doubtful about her ability to communicate in Spanish. Other informants sometimes stated that they felt conspicuous away from the market places in their traditional clothing when they traveled outside el Istmo.

Economic Spheres Open Only to Women

By investing time and labor in processing and selling the household production in small quantities, Isthmus Zapotec women are in a position to maximize the household income from that production. The more woman-hours a household can channel into processing and vending, the larger the household income. Extra woman-hours can always be shifted into processing and vending, even lacking production, simply by purchasing the raw products. Extra able-bodied adult women are probably always economically advantageous to the household while extra adult able-bodied men may or may not be, depending upon how much of their time is devoted to some activity which produces income. Men probably produce more income per man-hour than women when they are employed, but tend to be underemployed compared to women. That is, men have more leisure time and there are more apt to be considerable periods of time when they cannot work at productive activities because of weather, lack of skills, lack of a market (especially true for the labor market), and other reasons. In short, it is harder for men to find some way to turn a few pesos in slack periods and spare time than it is for women. The economic sphere in which women operate, processing and selling in very small quantities through the market places, in the street, or at home, is closed to Zapotec men by custom. When the women in the household cannot process and sell for whatever reason, income from agricultural production will decrease to the extent that it must be sold wholesale in its raw state.

Processing-Vending Related to Other Household Duties

The processing-vending role of women must compete with a multitude of other household tasks, of which the care of infants and toddlers takes precedence. Normally having learned her economic skills in her natal household, these are more or less held in reserve after marriage until the woman herself has a child or two old enough to share some of the burden of caring for children and household. Gradually, the young woman reactivates processing-vending skills she learned as a

Mother taking two babies and laundry to river to wash.

girl or develops new ones as opportunities present themselves. Young women with small children can earn a few pesos now and then if they must, but it is not until middle age that most women have a great deal of time to devote to income-producing activities. After about age sixty, failing health often curbs economic pursuits, but older women support themselves wholly or in part through vending as long as they are able. A rare elderly woman even supports herself by making and selling totopos regularly.

Tasks other than child care also demand attention from women of the household, cutting into the time which can be used to increase household income. But household tasks require rather less time in the Isthmus than might be expected, because of the tropical climate, cultural adaptations, and a few simple but significant technological advances such as the mechanical nixtamal mill which saves six or eight woman-hours daily formerly devoted to grinding by hand. The advent of manufactured textiles and sewing machines also saves many woman-hours previously spent in weaving and sewing by hand.[15] Probably the most burdensome household task is washing clothes by hand, but the amount of washing necessary

---

[15] Handweaving, formerly common among the Isthmus Zapotecs, has almost disappeared in the past generation. A few old women still weave in San Jacinto where handwoven skirt lengths can still be purchased. A few elderly Juanecas continue to wear the old-fashioned handwoven wraparound skirt.

for a family is greatly reduced by sleeping arrangements that require no sheets or other bedding (people sleep in hammocks or on woven mats), by the practice of drying the body with the hands after bathing and air-drying the hair which makes towels unnecessary, and by allowing babies and toddlers to go without clothing or diapers. Generally boys wear no clothing until they are five or six years of age except on special occasions and girls wear only a brief panty or skirt around the solar. Food preparation time is vastly reduced by mechanical maize grinding and the availability of ready-made tortillas and the whole range of other prepared foods the housewife can so easily and cheaply purchase from her neighbors. Most housewives prepare one "pot" per day, very often a *pasta* or rice-based stew with vegetables plus a few ounces of beef, fish, or shrimp added for flavor. Such a pot will feed the family for the main midday meal and the lighter evening supper, augmented by tortillas, *salsa*, coffee, sweet rolls, cheese, and other items purchased in the market to the degree that the household has cash available for these extras. In poor households the stew may contain no meat or other protein and only a few vegetables, and will be augmented only by tortillas.

The market places serve Isthmus Zapotec households in two important ways then: as a source of additional income and as a very inexpensive and convenient source of ready-to-serve food items, a device which saves labor just as packaged pre-cooked foods do in our own culture.

Dishwashing is never a great problem in Isthmus Zapotec households, although the amount of dishes and utensils used tends to increase with income and social status. In the campesino household, families with small children may not use individual dishes at all but simply dine in a circle around the cooking pot from which the parents feed themselves and the little ones, using tortillas as the utensil. At most, there will be a small bowl, cup, and perhaps a spoon for each individual. Teaspoons are needed only for stirring sugar into hot coffee as a rule. Tortillas serve as eating utensils as well as napkins to wipe one's mouth and finger-tips at the end of the meal. Unless the food is greasy, soiled dishes are merely rinsed in cold water and allowed to dry in the air. Grease is removed by adding a little soap powder to the water. The cooking pot will probably be left to soak until it is needed the following day.

Since the house itself usually consists of a single windowless room used mainly for storage of clothing and housing the *santa mesa* and since the average solar contains very little furniture, cleaning is not an especially time-consuming task. Most of the household's activities take place in the open, shaded patio called an *enramada*, or on the roofed open *corredor*, the same size and directly in front of the enclosed room. The corredor and enramada usually require sweeping daily since garbage and refuse are dropped randomly during the day's activities. The enramada floor is invariably packed earth and sometimes the corredor floor is also. Packed earth floors will be sprinkled by hand once or twice a day by the tidy housekeeper to confine the dust to a tolerable level. All in all, cleaning of the solar requires at most an hour per day. Again the amount of time household tasks require tends to increase with income and social status as houses become larger and furnishings become more elaborate. The traditional Isthmus Zapotec campe-sino solar, while neither comfortable nor aesthetically pleasing by North American standards, demands little time or attention from its occupants.

Animals kept within the solar or fed from the solar belong to the women of the household who also care for them. These include pigs, chickens, turkeys, and occasionally ducks but do not include oxen, although the latter are often kept within the house compound at night. Pigs may be penned in a corner of the solar but more commonly they are permitted to scavenge the streets, alleys, and river banks, returning to the solar to be fed scraps and a little maize in the evening. Usually the maize must be shelled by hand first, requiring as much as an hour if there are several large pigs. Chickens are also fed scraps and maize, but their care requires little time or effort since their numbers are few and they have the run of the solar. Chickens, the occasional eggs they produce, and pigs are rarely kept for household use. They are raised to be sold, and, for the women, constitute a source of cash for emergencies which they feel is worth the effort and inconvenience of their care. The men of the household sometimes complain about the pigs and chickens running about, saying it costs more to feed them than they are worth.

Ironing is a considerable task in some households and in others no ironing is done at all. This again depends on the income and social status of the household. The poorer campesino households have less clothing and what is owned is usually worn unironed except for special occasions.

Women are also responsible for nursing care of sick and disabled members of the household, a burdensome task over long periods of time and one which occurs with shocking frequency because of the general low level of health and lack of modern medical treatment for the majority of the population.

CONCLUSION

In concluding discussion of the division of labor by sex, the following points deserve emphasis:

1. Division of labor by sex is relatively strict.

2. Economic roles are generally complementary by sex.

3. Each sex has access to distinct spheres of economic actions not open to the other.

4. Men's economic roles are always considered more important than those of women, even in cases where the women's roles contribute the greater share to household income.

5. Because women have many other household duties which compete with and take precedence over income-producing activities, the latter are often short-term and intermittent as compared to those of men.

6. One result of women's processing-vending role is that men's production is sold by women in very small quantities over a period of time with the income spent immediately for food and other daily household requirements. To the extent that household production passes through women's hands, women are in a position to control the finances of the household, but in practice, day-to-day requirements of the household allow women little opportunity to employ such control advantageously, much less abuse it.

Juanecas sometimes use a phrase which I think typifies the Isthmus Zapotec woman's perception of her economic role. When she leaves the solar with something to sell in the market place she states, "Bueno, ya tengo que buscar la comida!," meaning she must sell what she takes to market in order to buy food for the next meal.

Women's Attitudes toward Processing-Vending

Despite the importance of the processing-vending role and the fact that some women obviously enjoy selling, Juanecas are ambivalent about the role. They invariably state that they find the role distasteful but an economic necessity. This ambivalence was demonstrated clearly when a small sample (forty-seven) processor-vendors was asked how they would dispose of a hypothetical windfall of a few thousand pesos. Only two women suggested expanding their processing-vending activities with the money. The others stated unequivocally that they would discontinue the role and simply stay at home, even though the proposed windfall was only sufficient to permit them to do so for a limited period of time, perhaps a year or two. Most women proposed spending the money on improvements to the solar.

This unexpected negative attitude toward the processing-vending role stems, I believe, from peasant women's acceptance of middle-class and elite mestizo values as the ideal. Local elite women seldom leave their solares, much less set foot in the market places. Servants do their shopping and errand running. On the rare occasions when they come to the central district, they are accompanied by servants to carry their purchases. Middle-class mestizo women may do their own shopping, but they never sell in the market places or on the streets.[16] They do not carry heavy burdens and never carry burdens on their heads, both more or less necessities for processor-vendors. Peasant women are acutely aware that their market activities mark them as "low class" to the mestizo population. They rationalize their economic role as a necessity of their unfavorable economic circumstances even when this may not be true in particular cases.[17] A second factor is the low esteem of marketing activities as compared with other economic roles. With few exceptions, marketing is thought of as an unskilled job anyone can do. Informants often state that they sell in the market "because my mother didn't teach me any skills" or "because I was an orphan and had no one to teach me anything." A relatively simple specialization such as seamstress commands great respect and is thought by most women to be much more difficult to master than is the case. This is probably because sewing machines, while not rare, are not available to every woman.[18] A third reason for the low prestige of processing-vending may relate to its small scale and consequent low level of profit for most vendors, but this would not explain why owning a tiendita is a status symbol although often less profitable than selling in the market places. Again, this seems to relate to the prevalence of mestizo values as ideals.

[16] Middle-class and even some upper-class women earn extra income by sewing, knitting, or selling Avon products, but they do so from their homes. One mestizo woman, an ex-schoolteacher, had begun selling Avon house to house part of the time, always accompanied by her husband.

[17] There are a few San Juan Evangelista families who are very well-to-do by regional standards, but the women continue the processing-vending role and continue carrying burdens on their heads even though such "low-class" behavior is not an economic necessity.

[18] Several San Juan women conduct sewing schools in their homes where girls are taught, for a fee, basic sewing techniques and the use of a treadle sewing machine. Seamstresses often train apprentices, which also involves an initial fee on the part of the apprentice. Seamstresses may employ from one to four apprentices, some of them young men.

Campesinos' Perception of Their Economic Position

Although Isthmus Zapotec campesinos are relatively more prosperous than are many other indigenous peasant populations in Latin America, they tend to think of themselves as economically and socially disadvantaged. A characteristic attitude of peasants in many parts of the world, this belief is often an accurate assessment of their situation. Yet Isthmus Zapotec peasants are well aware they are not on the bottom of the economic ladder even locally. There are certain types of work no Zapotec peasant will accept—for example, street peddling by men, laundering and housework by women. Destitute families will sometimes allow a daughter to accept a live-in position with a wealthy family, preferably in Mexico City. Such girls do not expect and will not tolerate treatment as servants. Unless they are treated as daughters of the family (and they are often related to the employing family), they will not remain no matter what the economic pressure. Well-to-do families in the Isthmus have a great deal of trouble acquiring and keeping satisfactory servant girls. The most prosperous San Juan households employ a servant or two when they can secure them, but prefer *vallistas*, who are harder working and less demanding. Laundresses, when they can be found, are almost always vallistas from the squatter settlements.

Zapotec peasants recognize as clearly beneath them two major groups: (1) the vallistas, which in local usage includes all the itinerant, rootless population which drifts in and out of the Isthmus, whatever their origin; and (2) the Mareños, the coastal peoples whom Zapotecs have dominated through trade relations for centuries.

Recognized as above themselves are the petty officials, clerks, schoolteachers, anyone who does not have to soil himself in his work or work with his hands.[19] Economically such persons are often far poorer than the well-to-do peasant families, but social status hinges on much more than mere economic resources. Clearly, the regional urban middle class and elites, even those of Zapotec origin, are all considered above the peasants on the social scale.

Actually, then, Zapotec campesinos occupy a middle position in the regional social status hierarchy, a position reflected in attitudes toward social inferiors but not in their perception of their status with respect to those above them.

[19] Even the use of the word *trabajo* is taboo in upper-class circles. Since I was a North American I was automatically placed as upper class. At first when people asked me, "What have you been doing today?," I replied, "working." One day an old man, head of one of the most prominent families in El Centro, took me aside. "Don't say you are working. That is such a vulgar word. Just say you are *paseando*," was his fatherly advice.

5 / Rhythms of Zapotec peasant life

For most individuals in every culture the day-to-day routine tends toward monotony and repetition. Isthmus Zapotec peasants are not exceptions. If anything, the eternal sameness of temperature, the ceaseless agricultural work cycle and marketing activities, and the paucity of recreational diversions add to the monotony of daily living. Boredom is especially trying for young people who have so few opportunities to use creatively youth's boundless energy and curiosity. But if there is a numbing tedium to daily life, there is also a sense of foreboding and insecurity which hovers over people's lives like a storm cloud on the horizon, promising to break the monotony—but in disastrous ways. This chapter introduces the reader to the basic rhythms of life—the life cycle and the daily routine, broken now and then by the annual ritual cycle and the rites of passage. The aspirations, anxieties, ideals, and values which shape people's behavior, adding flesh to the skeletons of life's routines, must be postponed to later chapters.

DAILY ROUTINE

For most households in San Juan Evangelista the day begins early, often well before daylight.[1] Coffee and sweet rolls or totopos break the night's fast with the main morning meal eaten around 7 A.M. after morning chores are completed and the day's tasks are ready to begin. This meal is almost invariably purchased in the local plazita because leftovers from the previous day cannot be consumed with safety. If the man of the house is going to the fields, he may have left at daylight, carrying food for the morning and noon meals, or if the distance is not excessive a child may be sent to the field later with a hot meal.

Women do the daily shopping immediately before or immediately after breakfast so that the food for the noon meal will have several hours to cook. If tortillas or totopos are to be made, a daughter of the house will take the grain, already soaked overnight, to the mill to be ground before breakfast. Women going to the El Centro market to sell will leave the house between 6 A.M. and 7 A.M. Those

---

[1] In the household where I lived for several months the regular hour was 4 A.M., about two hours before daylight. A number of households—for example, butchers of beef and pork—begin the day regularly between 1 A.M. and 2 A.M., while many others may do so from time to time in connection with specific activities such as going to el monte for firewood and lumber.

Midday meal in the field.

going to San Jacinto will probably not leave until 8 A.M. or 9 A.M. or even later, since that market is active all day. The woman who remains in the solar will tidy up, sweeping out the fruit rinds, pits, and other discards from the previous day and sprinkling the packed earth with water. She prepares the pot for the day and perhaps washes a few pieces of clothing. In some households, handling fruit and drying fish and shrimp are time-consuming daily chores.[2] Whatever time remains before the midday meal will be devoted to skills the woman possesses which provide income for the household—making tortillas, totopos, sewing *huipiles* by machine, embroidering, or perhaps making paper flowers. Girls between ten and fifteen who do not attend school will usually be put to selling something from the doorway or street corner near their home—homemade beverages, sliced oranges, cucumber or pineapple slices, mangoes, *gueezé*, or other snack foods. Boys of comparable age are more apt to be enrolled in school and to attend more or less regularly, but if not they will be helping their father with his tasks.

The midday meal is taken between 1 P.M. and 2 P.M. and is rarely a family affair. One or two persons may eat at the same time but it is more coincidence than

---

[2] For example, bananas are placed in a darkened room or storage space to ripen and must be turned daily. About every other day the ripe bananas must be selected from each stalk and removed to be sold or eaten. Drying fish and shrimp entails putting the products in the full sun, adding salt daily, and covering the drying tables at night with light cloths to keep off moisture and pests.

design. The man of the house and the sons will be served when they arrive home. Women and girls who remain at home eat when they are hungry and others eat when they return from the market place. Commonly a lone diner will not eat at a dining table, if indeed there is one in the household, but will seat himself on a *butaca*, using a regular straight-back chair for his table.

The afternoon siesta extends from the midday meal to about 4 P.M. for most people, but often people do not actually nap, or do so only for a short period. The remaining siesta time may be spent in visiting or doing some light sedentary work such as embroidery. If men are working far from the solar, they take the siesta in the field, not returning to the pueblo until dusk or later. If they are working near home they will probably try to complete their fieldwork for the day and return to the solar by siesta time, taking up some activity around the solar afterward.

After 4 P.M., when businesses reopen in El Centro and San Juan, household activities also pick up. Women who sell for the supper trade make preparations for going to the market place from which they will return about 8 P.M. Other women feed the household animals, carry firewood in for the morning, put grain to soak, and prepare the evening meal, which often entails only buying tortillas to go with the leftover midday stew. Water jars are filled if the solar has piped water. If not, boys will be sent to the nearest source from which water can be carried. Isthmus Zapotecs are personally fastidious people, normally bathing at least once daily. Women and girls often do this during siesta hours so that their thick hair, shampooed almost daily, dries before nightfall. Women bathe in the solar, dipping water from a large olla with half a gourd and pouring it over the body. Men will probably bathe in the river or irrigation canal on their way home from the fields, watering their oxen and washing both the oxen and cart at the same time. The man's last chore of the day is feeding his oxen, usually with fodder cut in the field and carried home on the oxcart.

Even if the solar has electricity, the family will probably retire at dusk or very shortly thereafter.[3] Artificial light is more useful in the cool hours before dawn when the day begins than in the evenings when everyone is tired and the day's heat lingers.

This routine is broken slightly on Saturday nights when young people stream to El Centro to attend one of the two cinemas and on Sunday evenings when they may join the *paseo* in El Centro. Otherwise Sundays are less exceptional than in many places because the market places remain open as do a number of El Centro businesses. Sunday mornings (as well as Thursday) find women and girls walking to the cemeteries with basins and buckets of fresh flowers on their heads to be left at the graves of loved ones. Sunday afternoons are traditionally the time when married daughters visit their mother's solar. Women who sell regularly in the market places do so seven days a week, taking an occasional day off as needed but usually not once a week and almost certainly not Sunday, the day market sales are best.

[3] According to the official 1960 census only slightly more than 5 percent of 1,130 households in the municipio had electricity, flush toilet, shower, and drain. In 1967 perhaps half of the households had electricity but the proportion of households with the four above-mentioned conveniences used as the criteria of modernity had improved only slightly.

The important breaks in routine are those marked by fiestas, whether honoring the saints or marking individual rites of passage. Women especially look forward eagerly to the fiestas, perhaps because they have almost no other socially acceptable form of recreation. Fiestas are the only occasions when it is permissible for women to dance, drink beer, gossip, show off their best clothing, and enjoy themselves in the company of other women outside a workaday context. Not only the fiesta itself, but preparation for it, which is often initiated a month prior to the fiesta, mean breaks in routine and social interaction for women. Even those women who are prevented from attending the fiesta itself because of mourning or other reasons can participate in the cooperative food preparation activities. Men sometimes complain that the womenfolk are too much involved in fiestas, and indeed they do contribute more cooperative labor and often more money than their menfolk.

Men often find recreation in drinking and conversation in the cantinas and around the peripheries of the fiestas, but men who attend fiestas seem to treat it less as recreation than ritual, a religious and social duty, a time for ritual drinking and cigarette smoking which inevitably ends in alcoholic stupor and probably, for most men, massive hangovers.

Market activities have often been mentioned as having recreational aspects for peasant women. There is no doubt that seasonal selling trips to Oaxaca or even simply to El Centro or San Jacinto provide welcome relief from routine for some women, and teen-age girls certainly anticipate trips to the market places or any other errands offering an escape from the solar, but I think the recreational, pleasurable aspects of market selling have been much overplayed with respect to Isthmus Zapotec women. Selling often involves a great deal of hard work, personal discomfort, and boredom which women would avoid if they could.

Young people seem to have less recreational opportunities than adults since the fiestas are ritual affairs of adult members of the community with youth having few formalized fiesta roles. Groups of teen-age girls or boys sometimes plan Sunday picnics in the orchards and more rarely at the beach. Occasionally mixed groups with chaperones hire a pickup truck and driver for a Sunday outing. Then there are the movie houses and Sunday night paseo attended mostly by the young people. The river, the pueblo's traditional playground, has lost its attraction in recent years because damming for irrigation and flood control has reduced it to a series of malodorous stagnant pools during much of the year.

THE LIFE CYCLE

There is little doubt that parenthood is one of the central values of Isthmus Zapotec culture. Without children neither women nor men can achieve true adult status, and the more children parents can successfully rear, the greater the chances of a secure old age for the parents.[4] One thirty-year-old informant ex-

---

[4] Raising children to adulthood is what counts. Often people forget to mention children under three years to census takers and other persons because they are not considered full members of the household until some time after age three. This oversight accounts for the population pyramid with a smaller base than would be expected, rather than a recent decrease in the birth rate.

Men watering oxen and bathing at day's end.

plained his lack of enthusiasm for fiestas with: "I have nothing against the fiestas. But how can I go and sit there all day among men when everybody knows I have no children! It makes me feel like a child myself!" Although unmarried, this man was head of the household of his widowed mother. One marries primarily to produce children and sterility is considered one of the greatest tragedies which can befall a woman.

Birth to Marriage

Pregnancies usually occur within a few months after marriage. Few taboos are observed. Unless one is ill, work is carried on as usual. Cheese and totopos are thought to be especially good for expectant mothers but there is little evidence that the normal diet is restricted or changed to a significant degree. There are no formal restrictions on sexual intercourse during pregnancy and in some cases at least it continues almost to the termination of the gestation period.[5]

---

[5] An informant expressed the opinion that Mongolian spots, a blue area which sometimes occurs at the base of the spine in newborn American Indian and Asiatic babies, were caused by the father's penis bruising the child before birth.

Babies are born at home with a local *partera*, close women relatives, and the father in attendance. The father's presence is of great importance and is in striking contrast to the general puritanical attitudes toward sex and modesty which prevail. The husband comforts and encourages his wife during labor, and after delivery it is the father's duty to place the afterbirth in a pottery jar which he then covers securely and buries under the floor of the house. If this is not properly done, the baby's eyes will become infected.[6] The parturient woman usually reclines on a canvas cot, but sometimes she assumes a half-reclining position on two benches placed a few inches apart. Local parteras without formal training charge $30 while those with some formal training may charge as much as $200. Medical doctors are not called unless complications arise and may charge up to $600. Very few women consult a medical doctor during pregnancy.

Shortly after birth the father may invite a few neighbors and friends for a little fiesta, especially if it is a first child or a first son. Mother and child rest on a cot while neighbors and relatives prepare and enjoy the fiesta.

Ideally mother and child do not leave the solar for 40 days but the mother usually resumes her normal household duties after about two weeks. Some families think it is important to have the baby baptized within the first month or two of life. A godparent of the same sex as the child takes the infant to the church for baptism without the presence of the parents. Other families put off baptism indefinitely as long as the child appears in good health, but he will eventually be baptized during the first four or five years of life. First communion is also variable. Some first communions take place as early as one month of age while others are postponed until the child is ten years old, often depending upon the availability of a willing sponsor. Again parents do not attend. Fiestas for baptisms and communions are rare, and when they occur, they are very small family affairs with only the godparent and perhaps a few other outsiders.

Babies are nursed for from one to two years nowadays and are not fed supplementally until they are at least a year old. The mother nurses the baby whenever it cries. As the baby's food demands increase beyond the mother's capacity to produce milk, the baby may become "fussy" and have to be nursed every few minutes, but the trouble is rarely diagnosed as hunger. Bottle feeding is rare, practiced only in extreme emergencies such as the death of the mother. It is never introduced as a supplement to breast feeding.

Although figures are absent, infant mortality is high in San Juan Evangelista; however, it has certainly dropped since the advent of antibiotics. The crucial periods are the first three months of life and the months after weaning, especially if weaning occurs as early as one year. Until age two or three, the possibility of

---

[6] A family who prided themselves on their modernity and lack of superstition had the extraordinary experience of the seventh child being born within hours after the grandmother died in the solar. As soon as labor commenced, the mother was removed to a nearby empty solar and attended by her youngest sister who had purposely stayed away from the solar until then so as to remain free from the contamination of *calor*. About three days after the birth they moved back into the solar. Meantime, the father had been prevented from burying the afterbirth because of his contamination. Once back in the home solar, the baby was placed under the continuous surveillance of the saint, *Corazon Sagrado de Jesus*. Nevertheless, the baby's eyes became badly infected, the first of the seven children to suffer such a fate.

death is a real one even today. The child's health is the direct responsibility of its mother, and when a death occurs, gossip circulates that the mother did not feed the child properly or that she neglected to protect it from the *calor* of the dead, from *ojo* or *aire* or other supernaturally caused illnesses. A prudent mother cares for the baby herself unless she has daughters old enough to share the responsibility. Children are rarely allowed outside the solar until they are about three years old.[7]

Isthmus Zapotec babies are never carried in rebozos as in other parts of Mexico but only in the arms or on the hip. The explanation probably lies in the practice of keeping babies confined to the solar. Except for frequency of nursing, infant care is relatively simple. No diapers are used but a piece of a discarded skirt is kept under the small baby to soak up moisture and protect his skin from the prickly *ixtle* hammocks and woven mats. These cloths can be quickly rinsed, dried, and reused so that only two or three are required. Mothers try to keep the genitalia of baby girls covered when men and boys are present. Otherwise no clothing is required. When a little girl is able to walk she will be dressed in homemade cotton panties. Boys normally wear no clothing until age six or so unless weather makes a light shirt mandatory.

Weaning between the ages of one and two is probably one of the leading factors in early childhood morbidity because a common result of early weaning is extreme malnutrition. I suspect that the short nursing period is a relatively recent development. The child of a year, unable to masticate his food, is weaned mainly on tortillas, *pozole, atole*, and coffee with sugar. His diet is certain to be almost totally lacking in proteins, calcium, and some critical vitamins such as Vitamin C until he is old enough to eat a wide variety of adult fare and then will be still deficient in protein and calcium. Although native local products which would provide an adequate diet are available and cheap (except milk), mothers are ignorant of nutrition and the effects of inadequate diet on children. They tend to blame childhood troubles on supernatural phenomena. As a consequence, the two-year-old child who was a chubby, bright-eyed infant a year earlier will probably be thin, suffering from recurrent diarrhea and fever, and exhibiting signs of rickets. Very often children between two and three years old suffer from open infected sores which may begin as nothing more than mosquito bites but because of malnutrition and low disease resistance are easily infected and slow to heal. The malady is thought of as a natural occurrence of childhood just as the ancient Greeks thought the symptoms of rickets were part of the normal development pattern. If a child's condition deteriorates or seems chronic, the mother, after having tried a series of folk remedies, will probably consult a medical doctor who invariably prescribes massive dosages of vitamins, some form of calcium (usually canned milk), an egg, and fresh tomato juice daily. Typically the vitamins will be administered until the baby shows signs of improvement if the family can afford them. The food products, so much cheaper and locally available, such as eggs and tomato juice, may be attempted once or twice, but if the baby rejects them they are discontinued because women see no connection between health and food as a source of vitamins purchased in bottles. But such severe cases of malnutrition should not be overstressed. Although common, not all infants exhibit symptoms of malnutrition.

[7] See footnote 4.

Differences between children are probably to be explained mostly by differences in weaning practices and family income and eating habits. One family with seven children, all in glowing health, began to buy canned milk for the two youngest after the older siblings learned in school of the importance of milk in the toddler's diet.

Toilet training is accomplished between the ages of two and three with little apparent effort. When the mother decides the child is old enough to understand her instructions, she explains where he is to go to urinate and defecate (usually a remote corner of the solar) and within a few weeks or months training is complete. If the child is slow to learn no pressure is put on him unless he proves inordinately slow when shame may be employed.

During the early years the mother and other female household members are mainly responsible for socializing the child because adult men are normally away from the solar during most of the child's waking hours. Although some informants claimed mothers were harsh disciplinarians, scores of observations of mothers and children of various ages in many different situations did not bear out the claim. The most severe action toward a small child I ever witnessed was a mild scolding. Two reports of severe beatings administered by mothers involved teen-age daughters. Informants were very critical of these actions by mothers, even though they acknowledged that the girls probably provoked the attacks by improper behavior. But these were extreme cases and obviously infrequent. Although some beating of wives and children by drunken husbands occurs, corporal punishment of children of any age by either parent is not condoned, nor is wife-beating. Isthmus Zapotecs are often overly permissive and benign in child training by North American middle-class standards. Children sometimes appear boisterous and unruly, but since they are largely confined to the solar, their behavior does not annoy the neighbors. A belief that children can become ill and even die of *tristeza* if they are harshly disciplined or not permitted to do as they wish is at least partly responsible for parental permissiveness.

Boys of all ages are allowed a great deal more freedom than are girls, and fewer demands and responsibilities are placed upon them and usually at a later age than for girls. If there are several younger children a daughter will begin to assume some responsibility for household duties by age six or seven. She will probably not be allowed to attend school because the mother depends on her help, especially if the family is poor. Care of infants and toddlers by older siblings occurs only within the solar and only under the close supervision of the mother or other adult. Children are never seen in the streets with infant siblings strapped to their backs as in some parts of Mesoamerica. Boys have few duties around the house, and the probability that they will attend school at least to age twelve or so is much greater than for girls. After age twelve the boy can begin to work in the fields with his father. The large majority of campesino families still considers even a minimal formal education for daughters an unnecessary frill, but that is gradually changing.

Girls begin very early to learn to be shrewd shoppers, to make change, and to add and subtract small sums mentally. By the age of seven, girls are sent now and again to the plazita to purchase food. When they return home, they must give an accounting of how much they paid for each item, along with the leftover change, to the mother. If she thinks the onion is too small for the price, the tomatoes of poor quality, or if the girl is short a tortilla (which sell fifteen for $1), the mother will probably scold her mildly. Sometimes a child will be sent back to the vendor to return an item and get a refund. Vendors, all Juanecas, are usually very tolerant of such exchanges and return the money without question. Gradually the girl gains enough experience to be sent to sell tortillas in the market place or sliced oranges from the doorway of the solar. This type of selling may begin as early as age ten. The money she earns is not hers but belongs to the household and is turned over to the mother. Boys, although they are often sent on errands by their fathers, do little buying and no selling, and therefore receive less experience in mental arithmetic than girls.

After age six, boys spend many hours playing in groups in the streets. Girls are seldom allowed to play outside the solar. Nor is it proper for older girls and women to be seen on the streets alone unless they are clearly on an errand. Girls are taught not to loiter on their way to and from the market place and are subject to reprimand if they do so. After puberty, girls are sent on fewer trips to the market places, especially during the early teens. Virginity at marriage is still expected, and although the girl's moral character reflects on the entire family, the daughter's behavior is mainly the mother's responsibility. In the early teens when girls are apt to be giddy and irresponsible they are kept under close surveillance "until she gets her reason" as the women explain it. During these years girls spend most of their time learning the more intricate household arts such as cooking and making tortillas and totopos, sewing, and embroidery. By the time a girl is seventeen she should be able to run her own household efficiently, although she will probably not have the opportunity to do so until some years after marriage. Relations between mother and daughter between puberty and marriage often become strained because of the tight restrictions placed upon the girl while younger children and older brothers enjoy much more freedom and less responsibility.

Although there are exceptions such as the family with five sons and one daughter, boys appear to be accorded preferential treatment by both parents in a number of ways. In education, parents are more willing to sacrifice for boys because sons are responsible for supporting aged parents. Sisters of whatever age are always subordinate to brothers until marriage. Observations based on perhaps a dozen families indicate that there is considerable rivalry between siblings of opposite sex, increasing as they grow to adulthood. Girls resent brothers because the boy has almost complete freedom just at the age when her movements are being severely restricted. Then, at the same time, the brother may take very seriously his responsibility for the good conduct of his sister, perhaps exaggerating the culturally sanctioned role as "protector" of his sisters until the girls view him as oppressor rather than protector. Again, the girl may resent the fact that family finances are being drained to educate a son while she works very hard with little reward helping the household meet such expenses.[8]

[8] One eighteen-year-old girl, within hearing of her mother, complained bitterly that all the mother's jewelry was going to pay for the medical education of her twenty-one-year-old brother, jewelry that would normally be part of her dowry. "By the time I marry we will all be paupers!" she lamented, not without cause perhaps.

Courtship and Marriage

From puberty until about age sixteen, girls are given very few opportunities to meet and talk with their age-mates of the opposite sex. Loitering or talking to boys in the streets is firmly discouraged, and every adult woman in the pueblo considers it her duty to report such misconduct to the girl's mother. When a girl is about sixteen, she will not be suddenly set free, but she will be allowed to attend a public fiesta on rare occasions where she will be under the watchful eye of an aunt or grandmother if not directly chaperoned. Younger siblings, cousins, or nieces and nephews often accompany teen-age girls even on errands. Finally the girl, accompanied by several of these young relatives, will be allowed to attend the Sunday evening paseos in El Centro on occasion.[9] The paseo in El Centro is a rather informal affair in which persons of all ages, even whole families, stroll around the plaza, those at the outer edge in one direction and those on the inner side in the opposite direction. There is much dropping out and visiting by couples with small children and middle-aged couples. Adults seem mostly to be mestizo middle-class couples from El Centro. The paseo attracts young people because it is about the only way one can look over the field of prospective novios and perhaps even manage to exchange a few words. This is the usual way courtships are initiated, although they sometimes begin by exchanges on the streets during those infrequent times girls are allowed out of the solar. Traditionally families arrange marriages but modern young people have more freedom to choose their own mates. Nonetheless, most courtships are slow, cautious affairs because the girl's parents may stop it at any point simply by confining the girl to the solar for an indefinite period, months perhaps.

After a few exchanges at paseos the boy will muster his courage sufficiently to wait in the street near the girl's home Sunday evenings until he finally hits an evening when she is being allowed to attend the paseo to which he accompanies her and her miscellaneous entourage of small chaperones. This is a critical point in the proceedings for the boy. No words need be exchanged, but if the girl allows him to accompany her, they are novios. The suitor hopes to keep the girl's parents from discovering his intentions until he is at least sure of the girl's feelings. If all goes well, he gradually becomes more self-assured and courageous enough to spend most of his free evenings waiting outside the girl's door out of sight in the hope that she will emerge on some errand. By this time the affair may have been in progress for months, perhaps more than a year. The girl's parents have long since become aware of the presence of the novio and given their tacit approval, all the while pretending total ignorance. Traditionally the courtship concludes with representatives of the suitor presenting a petition to the girl's parents on his behalf. The consent of the girl's parents initiated a series of ceremonial exchanges between the two families in the old days. Today the novio's father, godfather, or other adult male kin may talk to the girl's parents, but the ceremonial exchanges have been almost entirely abandoned. Once the courtship is initiated, breaking off

---

[9] The paseo derives from sixteenth-century Spain and still occurs in some Spanish peasant villages.

the affair by the couple themselves is considered unfortunate, especially for the girl because such an action is said to reflect on her character.[10]

Marriage banns are posted and announced over the public address system a month before the wedding mass. Since church weddings are not recognized by the Mexican government, the novios will probably be married *por civil* by civil servants in El Centro Saturday afternoon before the wedding. Brides wear their embroidered traje on this occasion rather than the bridal gown and may or may not be accompanied by their *padrinos*. If the parents are well-to-do, they may pay the civil officials to come to their solar Saturday afternoon where a small fiesta takes place after the civil ceremony.

All marriages in the church are performed at 8 A.M. mass on Sunday. In San Juan Evangelista as many as six couples may be married at this time, although one or two are the usual number. The novios are accompanied by their padrinos. As with baptisms, parents of the couple usually do not attend the wedding mass. At the end of the mass, each newly wed couple emerges from the church and pauses briefly for photographs previously arranged. A band is waiting just outside the gate, hired by the novio's father. As soon as the couple emerges from the church compound, their musicians strike up the local version of a wedding march and lead the newlyweds and padrinos, followed by the wedding party, through the streets of the pueblo to the home of the novio's parents. Even if cars and taxis are available, it is not proper for the newlyweds or the wedding guests to ride. Although the distance may exceed 2 miles, everyone walks. Their arrival at the virilocal solar, announced by a fiery barrage of *cohetes*, initiates a day-long "fiesta" which is actually a series of ritual acts performed by specific groups of persons at specific times, interlaced with intervals of dancing and beer drinking by the women and the drinking of *mezcal* toasts and cigarette smoking by men. The novios play an almost entirely passive role, seated all the long day at the novios' table flanked by the padrinos, rising only briefly at various times to perform their part of a ritual act such as kissing and passing to each guest a paper flower or kneeling to receive the benediction of the guests. Until midday the wedding guests are elder kinsmen and compadres of the novio's parents and *los invitados* of the padrinos. The bride's kin group arrives about noon and departs about two hours later, having fulfilled their part in the ceremonies. At about 4 P.M. the padrinos and their invited guests depart, leaving the newlyweds with the novio's kin.

Traditionally the marriage had to be consummated in the presence of witnesses, usually elderly female kin of the novio. That custom seems to have been completely discontinued in favor of allowing the couple more privacy, but the groom's kin group still expects to wait in the enramada until the consummation at which time the groom emerges to present his mother with a handkerchief stained with evidence of the bride's virginity. Then there is a great deal of excitement and rejoicing and the groom's mother heads a procession taking a basket filled with red flowers and containing the handkerchief to the bride's solar. The hour may be

---

[10] A middle-aged informant who considered that a novio had jilted her after initiating a courtship when she was fifteen years old still refused to speak to the man, although they both lived in San Juan Evangelista and frequently met on the streets or at fiestas by chance.

Leaving a wedding fiesta, a woman holds a bowl of mole *topped with a tortilla,
a gift of the hostess to every woman guest.*

Los invitados *going to wedding fiesta.*

late but the band leads the way as cohetes mark the procession's departure. Mercifully, the newlyweds are spared this final procession. The bride's kin group, especially the women led by her mother, will celebrate with a fiesta of their own Monday, at which time girls pass through the market places with baskets of red flowers, sprinkling red confetti on the heads of vendors and customers alike as an announcement of a successful conclusion to the marriage rites.

The more or less public consummation of the marriage and the great publicity which accompanies it in the traditional ceremony are considered by most young people a horrendous ordeal. For the girls especially it is a traumatic experience they never forget, but boys too prefer to avoid it. Fortunately there is an alternative in the form of marriage *por robar*, or elopement. No statistics are available, but my impression is that the number of elopements at least equals the number of traditional marriages. Again I cannot state whether this is a stable condition of some duration or whether elopements are becoming more prevalent than formerly.

Elopement involves the couple agreeing secretly to meet at a designated time and place. They go to the novio's home where he hides the girl from his parents as long as possible, usually a few hours. When the parents discover the elopement, they go immediately to talk with the girl's parents—even if the hour is 3 A.M.—

to persuade her parents to accept an arrangement. If they are agreeable, the girl may return home the next day and begin making preparations for a church wedding a month hence. If the parents are opposed the couple will probably remain together, hoping for a later reconciliation with her parents.[11]

Some elopements end in common-law marriages, other couples are eventually married *por civil* only, and still others marry by church and civil ceremony, both some time after the elopement. Matrons take great pride in claiming marriage *por los dos lados*, which is a mark of status. Most common-law couples never admit to their children that they are not married in the church and by law, and it is not rare for couples secretly to complete these ceremonies after ten, twenty, or more years of common-law marriage, usually when some legal matter makes it imperative.

When the bride goes to the solar of her husband immediately after the marriage, she goes to her new home where the couple will remain perhaps until two or three children are born, perhaps until the old people die and the husband inherits the solar. The first years of marriage can be an uncomfortable time for a young wife in a strange household under the thumb of a mother-in-law who may have been a complete stranger to her. Some brides cannot adjust and persuade their husband to establish a neolocal residence as soon as possible. Although divorce is not recognized by the church, it is possible according to the law of the republic. Some brides take this route to freedom after failing to persuade the husband to make a new home. The bride and her children, if there are any, return to her natal home where it is her brother's responsibility to provide for her. Divorce is still uncommon in San Juan Evangelista but is frequent in El Centro. Women are also learning that they can petition the courts for child support from the father even if there was no marriage ceremony, and they are not shy about doing so.

A surprising number of wives do adjust remarkably well to living with their mothers-in-law, however, and sometimes very strong bonds of affection form between them over the years. Frequently mothers-in-law side with the wife against their own son, especially when his behavior is obviously at the root of the trouble. Padrinos of the newlyweds are supposed to act as advisers and mediators between the couple all of their married life. In event of serious problems, the padrinos will probably be called in to arbitrate before legal action is taken by either side.

A wife's status increases as her family grows, reaching its highest when she herself becomes a mother-in-law to her sons' wives. A woman without daughters-in-law is unfortunate because she will be either left alone in old age or have to depend on her daughters. If all the daughters are married there is a conflict of duties. Care for the husband's aged parents takes precedence ideally but not always in practice. Elderly parents worry a great deal about nursing care in old age which is often required and must be provided by members of the household.

---

[11] An elder daughter of a large family eloped with only six weeks of school remaining before she was to graduate with a secondary diploma. The family had made great sacrifices for her education and was vastly disappointed. The couple did not contact the parents for three months, hiding out in the novio's solar in another town. Reconciliation had to wait the birth of the first child more than a year later.

In Zapotec culture elders of both sexes are highly respected and treated with great courtesy. No parent is willfully neglected, and parents normally retain a great deal of authority over their families as long as they live, especially over those who live in the parents' solar.

The best period of life for the individual begins in middle age, for this is the time when children begin to help substantially in supporting the household, the time when parents may have more time and money to devote to the fiesta system and making various *promesas* and commitments which will add to status and prestige. For women, at least, freedom from some of the severe cultural restrictions begins in middle age after the childbearing years end. As the woman grows older, she can go anywhere alone, attending fiestas as often as she wants and can afford, and she has daughters-in-law and grandchildren to augment her status. For the first time, women and men are more or less equal in status and prestige because age rather than sex becomes the determinant. Men's and women's roles are not as sharply drawn as previously and the sexes are allowed free interchange for the first time in their lives. Elderly men and women, perhaps lifetime compadres or neighbors and later widowed, lend one another comfort and moral support during the trying periods of illness and death. These tender relationships between the aged are among the most poignant in Isthmus Zapotec culture.[12]

Death and Rituals for the Dead

Isthmus Zapotecs do not have North Americans' exaggerated aversion to death. Indeed, it is possible that Isthmus Zapotecs are more preoccupied with death than is generally true in Mesoamerica, although the subject is very much a part of everyday thought and habits everywhere. In el Istmo, death is no stranger even to small children, who hear their elders discuss and refer to it every day in numberless contexts. Not unexpectedly, a great deal of ritual centers around death and honoring deceased kin. Dead kin, especially parents, continue to exert great influence on the living, not infrequently receiving as much attention as during life. Women are especially attentive to deceased parents and husbands, carrying flowers to their graves once or twice a week sometimes for years. Households often undertake heavy financial burdens to fulfill obligations to deceased members through the series of *mixa guétu*.

Although natural causes of illness and death are recognized, prevalent beliefs center around strong emotions such as fright and anger, witchcraft, evil eye, los aires, spirits, calor of the dead, and the imbalance of hot and cold influences on the body's humors.[13] Most people try home remedies first. If there is no improvement in the condition, women usually call a *curandera* for themselves and their

[12] An elderly woman, bedridden for a year, was visited by an old man, a neighbor of years long past, whom she had not seen for several years. The sickroom was full of family and several other visitors. The old man spent the better part of an hour leaning over his former neighbor, whispering in her ear, after which he greeted the other persons briefly and departed. I witnessed a number of similar instances of tenderness, concern, and confidence between nonrelated elderly persons of opposite sex, especially when one of them was in poor health.

[13] Most of these beliefs derive from sixteenth-century Europe but some elements may have been similar in both the Old World and the New World folk beliefs.

children. She diagnoses the cause of the illness and then treats it accordingly. Often a medical doctor or a druggist is consulted also, especially the latter who prescribes the medicines he sells. Illnesses that do not respond to any of these treatments are most likely to be attributed to supernatural causes still not diagnosed, and efforts are continued to seek the responsible supernatural agent. Men are thought to be more immune to many of the supernaturally and emotionally caused ailments than are women and children and therefore do not consult native curers often.[14] As an informant put it, "We [women and children] need the curanderas a lot because we are desirable. We get sick so much because people are always admiring us." Men are not thought to be attractive and desirable in the same way as women and children, but they too sometimes suffer illness caused by anger, fright, witchcraft, and spirits of the dead. Men are prone to consult the druggist for medicine after home remedies fail, then medical doctors, but the women of the household will probably prevail on them to consult native curers too, especially if improvement is slow. Recently people have begun to look upon the antibiotics as miracle drugs, using them indiscriminately for the smallest cause.[15]

No Zapotec lives alone or dies alone by choice, and few do so by chance. While ill persons and babies are protected from direct or indirect contact with corpses because they are adversely affected by the calor of the latter, sick people are never isolated from other persons because they are sick. Indeed, there seems to be a conscious effort to include the gravely ill member in all of the household affairs by placing him in a central spot where he can observe and hear everything. Inevitably a visitor to the household, even a complete stranger, will be ushered into the solar and presented a seat where the invalid can see and hear the visitor. In view of the general suspicion which surrounds strangers, I found this custom unexpected. Perhaps the stranger is not viewed as a danger to a dying person because desire, admiration, and envy are thought to be absent.

When death seems imminent, relatives and neighbors, including children except babies, crowd around the dying person, the women weeping, leaning over the victim to detect and observe signs of respiration. This knot of people around a dying person is sometimes so dense that breathing is difficult for a normally healthy person caught in the press of bodies. As soon as death is positive, women's quiet weeping changes to loud wailing interspersed with stereotyped mourning expressions. At the same time the scene takes on a sense of urgency, for there are many things to be arranged immediately even under a cloud of deep mourning. Someone not of the immediate household, often a female neighbor or distant relative, prepares the body by dressing it, binding the arms and legs, and placing coins on closed eyelids.[16] Members of the family, usually the eldest male members, must make arrangements for a burial space in the crowded graveyard, order a

[14] The majority of native curers are women. The only male curer known to me personally, although informants knew of others, rarely if ever treated people but specialized in curing solares. All informants denied that curers or curing rites were employed for animals, but I learned of one case of a mestizo in El Centro hiring a curer for his dog.

[15] Most drugs, as well as hypodermic equipment, can be purchased without prescription. A few practical nurses specialize in giving shots for a small fee, so that people can obtain antibiotics and have them administered intravenously without consulting a medical doctor.

[16] Informants disagree as to whether or not corpses are bathed.

casket to be delivered within a few hours, and hire a band to begin playing soon after the body is laid out. Women make preparations for the many accouterments of death—the great candles, flowers, river sand, items of clothing, a white sheet for a shroud, incense, and a new *petate*. Prayer leaders and women to supervise the preparation of food must be contacted and given orders, and the priest must be hired to give the funeral mass. In some households the place where the person died and everything in contact with the person at the time of death is placed in quarantine for eight days, locked up or otherwise isolated to contain the calor of the dead and render it harmless.

Mourning men of the family wear an armband of black satin while all the women and girls of the household immediately don total mourning (all black) which includes covering the head with a black cloth or rebozo and keeping it covered for eight days. A large bow of black satin is fashioned and hung over the outside entrance to the solar to announce the death to passersby. This sign of mourning is never removed. Faded to a ghostly gray and whipped by the relentless windblown sand, it will ultimately hang in shreds as a reminder of the household's period of sadness. The condition of the black satin over the entrance is a reliable indication of the length of time since a death last occurred there. Elaborateness and cost of the burial clothing vary with the economic condition of the family. Persons of both sexes are dressed mostly in black, the men with white shirts and black trousers. A poor woman will probably be dressed in a mourning costume she has worn while living; a more affluent woman, in a new and costly outfit of black lace or black velvet with white lace *olan* and *huipil grande*. Sometimes the woman of the house or the deceased herself has made a number of these preparations in advance such as having her burial clothing made to order, purchasing a white sheet, and ordering the candles made, as Doña Rufina did while I was living in her solar.

Once the corpse is prepared it is placed on a folded mat over a bed of clean river sand on the floor of the house, feet pointing toward and in close proximity to the santa mesa. Two adobe bricks are placed under the head of the deceased as a pillow and two or three white handkerchiefs are unfolded and placed over the face. The 3-foot-tall candles of beeswax and vases of fresh flowers flank the corpse at whose head a little dish containing cornmeal and another with burning incense are placed.

The formal mourning ritual begins as soon as the corpse is placed before the santa mesa. Women gather behind the corpse, facing the santa mesa, kneeling on mats while a *rezadora* leads the prayer chants and an elderly man carefully and profusely incenses all around the body and the santa mesa with *copal*. These prayer sessions, or *rosarios*, will be repeated continuously until burial, each lasting about a half-hour. The women of the household are expected to spend most of these long hours on their knees in the prayer sessions, but they rest from time to time by sitting on a bench. At the end of each rosario women pay their *limosna* to the female head of the household as they leave. For men and children, mourning is much less strenuous. Male members enter to pay their respects from time to time, kneel and say a prayer before the santa mesa, but they are mainly occupied in the enramada near the "men's santa mesa" to receive male neighbors, compadres,

Pottery vendor wearing mourning.

and relatives who pay their *cuotas* and are given a mourning toast of mezcal or *anisado*. Children are not much restrained and may go about freely observing all the activities. A baby or an ill household member may be taken to the solar of a relative or neighbor when death is imminent so that he may escape exposure to the calor.

Musicians, who sit in the enramada, sometimes play from death until burial in the intervals between the rosarios. At other times they are only hired to play at the time of burial, beginning shortly before the corpse is taken to the church.[17]

The tropical climate and absence of embalming make burial within twenty-four hours almost mandatory. If there is a few hours' delay pending arrival of close relatives from distant places, the corpse will be removed from its sand bed and placed on a mat over blocks of ice. The time of the burial is conditioned by hour of death. If death occurs in the hours before dawn, burial will probably take place by 4 P.M. of the same day. At the appropriate time the corpse will be lifted from its bed of sand and placed in the casket, then carried to the church for mass, and then borne to the cemetery which by law must be a considerable distance from the church. In San Juan Evangelista the cemetery is nearly two miles from the main church. Even if vehicles are available, the burial procession always proceeds on foot, with two or three extra pallbearers to relieve the six regulars at intervals. Sometimes close women relatives do not go to the cemetery but continue mourning at the rosarios before the santa mesa where the bed of sand remains during the eight days of the *novena*, either shaped into the form of a cross or left in the approximate outline of the corpse, and covered with fresh flowers and petals. At the graveside a short prayer session takes place, then mourners participate in throwing the first bits of earth on the casket in the grave.

When the burial party returns from the cemetery, a meal awaits them and other mourners, regardless of the hour. This meal takes on some of the character-istics of a fiesta as the women chat and gossip and the men imbibe in their corner of the enramada before and after the meal, sometimes relating humorous stories. In some cases there seems to be a deliberate attempt on the part of guests to turn the mourning family's attention from the death by light and inconse-quential conversation.

The rosarios continue every evening for eight days in the solar of the deceased, with neighbors, friends, and relatives joining the family. Early in the morning of the ninth day the household members and perhaps a few of the immediate family members not in the household gather the sand, dry flower remains, fresh flowers, candles, and the two head bricks and walk to the cemetery where the bricks are placed at the head of the new grave and the sand is sprinkled over the surface and covered with the dry and fresh flowers. At death the spirit of the deceased did not immediately reach its final destination but journeyed for eight days, the reason for the eight-day period of intense mourning and prayer.[18] The

---

[17] When the musicians arrive and how long they play are conditioned by family finances. If money is no object, two or three bands may be hired to provide almost continuous music from the time the body is laid out until after the burial feast. Death in a truly destitute family may be entirely without music. I knew of only one such case, the adult crippled son of a widow.

[18] Some informants claim the spirit of the deceased lingers around the solar for eight days

river sand and the head bricks have "soaked up" the sins of the deceased while the corpse lay in contact with them and are purified by the novena rites. The general body of beliefs about death is part of a Mesoamerican pattern deriving in part from the indigenous pre-Conquest religions and in part from sixteenth-century Catholicism.

During the forty days following a death, the women of the mourning household leave the solar as infrequently as possible. Selling in the market place is taboo although purchasing is permitted. Men, on the other hand, are free to take up their occupation immediately if they so desire and at most remain in the solar for a day or two after burial of the deceased. At the end of forty days the first and most important mixa guétu is held, terminating the period of intense mourning.[19] This consists of hiring a priest (sometimes two or three) to say a memorial mass at the church in honor of the deceased after which relatives and invited guests gather in the mourning family's solar for a fiesta.[20] A guest list of 200 persons or more is not unusual but there is great variation, the smallest having only two or three dozen invited guests.

The Wearing of Mourning by Women

The observant visitor to el Istmo will probably note that a great many women and girls wear mourning. This is not necessarily a reflection of an extraordinarily high mortality rate but of the wide circle of kin and fictive kin for which mourning is worn and the length of the mourning period. For parents, women wear full mourning at least one year and semi-mourning another year.[21] There is no limit to extension of the mourning period if the mourner desires. Widows, especially those past middle age, often wear mourning for the remainder of their lives. Grandparents and siblings usually command at least six months' full mourning and six months of semi-mourning, and women usually wear full mourning from six months to one year for compadres who were padrinos to their children. Besides genuine attitudes of respect toward the deceased, the fear of censure through gossip assures that an appropriately lengthy mourning period will be observed. Women feel that they make a sacrifice by wearing mourning because it is uncomfortable, unattractive, and usually requires more washing than regular clothing. In addition, the woman or girl in mourning is supposed to act properly sad and subdued and cannot attend fiestas or other public events. It is not unusual

---

to see if the family is honoring it properly. Others state that it travels for eight days on a hazardous journey. A spirit which is discontent for some reason, a quarrel with someone or an unfulfilled vow to a saint, or because death was violent and accidental, may linger on the premises for weeks or return later to haunt relatives. Therefore, much care goes in to performing the rituals properly and making the rites as opulent and lavish as circumstances allow.

[19] If the funeral fiesta has been elaborate, the forty-day mixa guétu may be small and vice versa.

[20] *Fiesta* as the term is used throughout this case study refers to a ritual meal or series of such rituals. It is not necessarily a joyous occasion.

[21] Full mourning is all black, semi-mourning is either black or navy blue with small, simple decorative touches permissive, especially skirts of small white figures on black or navy blue background, and blue instead of black ribbons in the hair.

for a woman to be in mourning for several years at a time as one elder relative after another succumbs. Unmarried girls find mourning frustrating, especially for aged great-uncles, and great-aunts, and padrinos, during the years the girls are searching for a husband. In such cases the girl's complaints might persuade her mother to shorten the mourning period. Sometimes a woman will take a vow to observe some additional mourning rite for a certain period of time for a husband or parent. An informant vowed to wear a black head cloth for the first six months after her mother's death in addition to regular full mourning.

After the first mixa guétu usually two more rites are celebrated during the first year after death. There will be an open house in the solar on *Todos Santos* November 2 when offerings will be made to the deceased at the santa mesa and at the grave.[22] The first anniversary of death is celebrated with another mixa guétu very similar to the one after forty days and sometimes the most elaborate of all. The formal mourning period ends with the first anniversary fiesta, but the anniversary date may be marked the third and seventh year by additional mixa guétu.

In summary, Isthmus Zapotec culture is heavily laced with rituals and activities centering around the dead. One might perhaps view the people as practicing ancestor worship since the most elaborated death rituals focus around parents and elders. The deaths of small children require simpler and more private family rites while newborn and stillborn infants are usually buried without any public ritual.

[22] Contrary to the custom in Mesoamerica generally, Todos Santos is not a day when every household honors the dead by making offerings in the cemetery. Some do this but it is mainly those households where a death has occurred within the past year. The general time of honoring all dead ancestors is the Easter season for the Isthmus Zapotec. In San Juan Evangelista the Thursday before Easter is customary. In San Jacinto Ash Wednesday is observed in one cemetery and Palm Sunday in the other. These are times when literally every family goes to the graves of its deceased kin with food for the living as well as the dead, spending the entire night in the cemetery. A temporary market springs to life in front of the cemeteries where all kinds of food, drink, flowers, everything for the living or the dead for this occasion is sold; there is music and visiting. It is not a gay time but neither is it sad.

6 / Religion and ritual

THE FIESTAS

After the Conquest there developed in many indigenous communities of Mesoamerica a system whereby religious and local political offices were combined and arranged in a hierarchical order. Usually the *cargos* were for terms of one year, becoming more costly to the holder as well as more prestigious as he moved up the cargo ladder. Although civil and religious offices now must be separated according to the law of the Republic of Mexico, there are a few indigenous communities where the old cargo system continues to function much as it has since colonial times.[1] In most places, however, changes in the system have been profound, sometimes to the point of extinction. In el Istmo there exists today a full calendar of fiestas, some of which had their origins in the older system, others of more recent origin. The nature of the fiestas varies from those which are still considered primarily sacred rituals to completely secularized events for entertainment purposes. All are called "fiestas" except the masses for the dead and the attendant ritual meals. San Juan Evangelista is a community in which parts of the cargo system continue to be important as means of achieving and maintaining status and prestige, although the character of the system is changing from an emphasis on public, community-centered fiestas to private, household-centered fiestas concerned with marriages and death rites. Political and religious offices have long been separated here, the former now elective and appointive, the latter voluntary. In order to distinguish the present system as it exists in San Juan Evangelista from the older system, I shall refer to it as the fiesta system, in which death rites are included.[2]

The emphasis in the following pages focuses on the meaning of the fiestas to the participants in terms of social status and prestige. Description of the events of the fiestas will be of minor concern.

Community-centered Fiestas

The public, community-centered fiestas, on which the old cargo system was built, centered around religious duties and honoring of the patron saints. In early

---

[1] See Cancian 1965 for a detailed account of a cargo system which still maintains its functional integrity.

[2] "Fiesta system" as employed herein refers to a ceremonial or ritual system. Secular fiestas are not included and indeed are still absent in San Juan Evangelista, although they are the prevalent type in some parts of El Centro and in some other towns of the Isthmus.

colonial times Catholic padres supervised the construction of churches and cathedrals, each dedicated to a particular saint (or saints) who served as its patron. A sizable town would have a cathedral, whose patron saint was the patron of the entire community, and a series of churches, often one in each barrio, again each with its patron saint representing that particular barrio or neighborhood. Usually the town and the barrio were referred to by the name of the patron saint, or the older name was retained and the saint's name added to distinguish communities with the same patron saint.

The traditional public fiestas of the Isthmus Zapotecs were noted for their length and elaborateness. In general, they consisted of a series of events covering five or six days, each beginning with a public procession through the pueblo by the *mayordomos* and others directly connected with the events of that particular day and ending in a *vela*, a festival which included music, dancing, and food and drink in the home of the mayordomo. Most public fiestas included a *Convite de Flores* (which can be translated as "reunion of the flowers"), a procession of men and boys in oxcarts laden with flowers, banana leaves, palm leaves, and often an entire banana plant, the oxen themselves decorated with collars of flowers and leaves.[3] The procession of oxcarts ended in front of the church where the carts were emptied of their contents in wild chaos of men, oxen, carts, music, and fireworks. Another fiesta event was the *Tirada de Frutas*, usually occurring late Saturday afternoon. This began with a procession of unmarried girls in their finest hand-embroidered trajes and gold jewelry parading through the streets with *jicalpextles* of fruit on their heads. The procession ended at the church where the girls either climbed up through the belfry of the church and emerged on the roof or climbed to a platform erected for them in the churchyard. From there they threw their fruit, piece by piece, including heavy papayas, pineapples, and coconuts, and small favors such as paper flags and novelties, into the crowd of children and young men waiting below. Sunday marked the mass in honor of the patron saint and the last day of the fiesta proper. Monday was a special fiesta for the women who had worked preparing and serving the food throughout the long fiesta. This was called the *Lavado de Ollas* or "washing the pots" but there is little indication that any great quantity of pots was actually washed. Usually this was a daytime fiesta attended almost entirely by women but not limited to the workers only. It was the only occasion when it was permissible for women to drink to the point of inebriation.

The velas, each with a name which was often that of an animal, began in the late afternoon each day of the fiesta and continued to the small hours of the morning, sometimes until sunrise. Each year different households were chosen to sponsor the velas, each a separate vela. San Juan Evangelista's "Fiesta Titular" had five velas of which only the first is still performed. Older informants remember the sequence of the velas and their names, although all five have not been performed for about twenty-five years.

Today the fiestas in San Juan Evangelista still incorporate the Convite de Flores, the Sunday mass, the Tirada de Frutas, and the Lavado de Ollas, as well

---

[3] Formerly sugar cane played a substantial role in the Convite de Flores.

Musicians lead the fiesta procession, followed by men on horseback.

as a procession each day and a *baile* several afternoons and evenings. High prestige still accrues to those households who volunteer to act as mayordomos. Sometimes there is only one sponsor for the entire fiesta, sometimes there are two or three households which share the burden, each sponsoring a particular day's events. In 1967 a committee sponsored one of the public fiestas (the pueblo has two patron saints) through donations from citizens and various fund-raising devices, and the other fiesta had three mayordomos. Acting as mayordomo can still be a large and costly affair requiring the sponsors to burden themselves with heavy debts for several years afterward.[4] Therefore, sponsorship is not undertaken lightly or frequently.

Many ritual acts, including sponsorship of fiestas by individuals or households, represent the fulfillment of a promesa made to the saint during a personal or familial crisis. For example, if a child is near death, the parents may vow to a saint that if the child recovers, they will sponsor a fiesta in honor of the saint as payment for his divine intervention. If the child recovers, the parents must make good their promise, although it may take years to accumulate enough wealth

[4] Mayordomos of a public fiesta in 1965 spent about $18,000, of which approximately $7,000 was contributed by others. Compare this to the daily wage of a farm laborer at that time, $10, or the cost of building a first-class traditional dwelling, $20,000.

Las señoras *in their* trajes *and* huipiles grandes *follow the men's contingent in fiesta procession.*

to do so. Of course, if the parents were poor, with no hope of ever accumulating that amount, they would make a lesser promesa, one whose fulfillment was possible while still representing a substantial sacrifice. The kinds of promesas that are made and the cost of fulfilling them, both financially and in personal effort or discomfort, range from acting as mayordomos, through undertaking long pilgrimages to the shrine of a particular saint, to simple acts such as burning candles to a saint daily for a certain period of time. Highest prestige is accorded those who sponsor public fiestas to the patron saints because this is seen as a benefit to the entire community; that is, they are paying the expenses so that the entire community can honor the patron saint.

I have stated that households sponsor fiestas. Normally the man and his wife, the household heads, are referred to as the mayordomos. The role of each sex is so vital that if a man is unmarried, his mother, sister, or other close female relative

Women dancing the zandunga *at wedding fiesta. The inebriated man is behaving improperly and will soon be led away.*

will be chosen to act as mayordoma. Or if the household has no male head, the woman acts as the mayordoma and chooses a close male relative to fill the role of mayordomo. In this case, the fiesta will be said to have had a mayordoma rather than a mayordomo, and the honor and prestige will accrue to the mayordoma and her household rather than to the person whom she chooses for mayordomo. Such cases are not unusual, although fewer women sponsor fiestas alone than couples simply because households without male heads are relatively rare, especially those able to sponsor such a costly event.

Today only a small percentage of households in San Juan Evangelista is willing or able to sponsor public fiestas, even in return for the attendant high prestige and status. Alternate routes to status are becoming acceptable, while some "progressives" actually speak out against the public fiestas as great wastes of money and effort. But many people, especially those not quite wealthy but affluent and upwardly oriented, firmly believe that the mayordomo route is the only acceptable means of establishing a high status for the household.

Family-centered Fiestas

Most of San Juan's nearly 1,200 households can never hope to sponsor a public fiesta, but there are still many ways households can add to their status and prestige

Women's group of wedding procession. Elder in foreground is a trailing member of men's contingent.

through the fiesta system. They can host family-centered fiestas such as weddings and mixa guétu, act as padrinos at baptisms, communions, and weddings, participate as invited guests at the fiestas of others, and make voluntary contributions. Each of these four classes or degrees of participation involves expenses and reciprocal obligations.

Hosting Family-centered Fiestas

Acting as hosts at private fiestas does not involve the fulfillment of a promesa to a saint, nor does the household have much choice about when they will give a private fiesta since these involve marriages and deaths as they occur. At most a household might have a year to plan and save toward the event. Therefore, prestige does not accrue so much for hosting a private fiesta as it does for "making a good showing" at those the household must give in terms of number of invited guests and quantity of food, drink, and music. A large private fiesta can be as costly as sponsoring a public fiesta, although that is the exception.[5]

Status through Compadrazgo

Another prestige-gaining activity is that of sponsorship of children at baptism, communions, and marriage. In order of prestige, sponsorship at baptisms and at

---

[5] See footnote 4. The most elaborate wedding in many years cost the novio's father something over $20,000 in 1967.

marriages is greatest while sponsorship at communions is of minor importance. Sponsoring a child's baptism involves buying the baby's baptismal gown, a candle, and perhaps some memento such as gold earrings for a girl, and paying the church's fee of $10. Altogether a baptism costs the sponsor not more than about $200 initially. Acting as padrinos of a marriage entails a greater cash outlay for buying or renting the bridal gown and accessories, and sponsoring and paying for a part of the wedding fiesta, averaging a total of $1,000 for a "nice" but not opulent wedding. The obligations incurred at the time of sponsorship are only the beginning of the padrino's obligations to the child or couple and their parents. Each of these acts establishes a lifelong ritual kinship between the padrinos and their *ahijados* and between the padrinos and the parents of the ahijados, who become compadres to each other. For this reason, compadrazgo carries much prestige to the sponsoring couple but is limited by their capacity to fulfill the obligations of a growing number of such relationships. Most parents in San Juan Evangelista choose for their children padrinos who are socially equal or a little better than themselves and who are also residents of the pueblo but are not close relatives. From this clue one may correctly deduce that the people of San Juan think it is most important to enlarge and strengthen their social relationships within their own community and among more or less social equals. This is not to say that compadrazgo ties are never established outside the pueblo or between socially unequal households. Both occur infrequently.[6] Informants were unanimous in stating that the sponsoring compadres occupy the most prestigious end of the relationship and that the parents of the sponsored children as well as the children themselves always owe the padrinos respect and gratitude for accepting such an obligation. Sponsorship is neither asked nor accepted lightly. An average couple will act as padrinos only two or three times in a lifetime; a poor couple with many children, perhaps once or never, while a prosperous couple may eventually establish a dozen or more compadres through sponsorship.

Participation in Fiestas as Invited Guests

Invitations to private fiestas are normally extended to a wide circle of real kin, to all compadres of the hosts, to persons the hosts "owe" by reason of previous invitations, and to persons with whom the hosts wish to establish reciprocal relations in the future. The more status the household possesses, the more often will the couple who heads it be invited to fiestas of others, and the more fiestas to which the couple is invited (and attends), the more their status is enhanced. Wedding fiestas include two groups of invited guests, those of the hosts and those of the padrinos, both approximately equal in status. Invited guests are almost always married adults (exceptions are middle-aged and older persons who have never married and widowed persons), and most invited guests at any particular

[6] The compadrazgo system, so much a part of Latin American culture, can be utilized in various ways to strengthen and extend particular types of social relations—between biological kin, between families of unequal social status, between distant trading partners, between nonkin of equal status, and other ways. See Mintz and Wolf 1950 for a concise analysis of compadrazgo.

fiesta will be elders, individuals who have spent many years incurring and paying ritual obligations in the fiesta system.

Invited guests must contribute a suitable amount to the hosts, $3 to $5 for women and $5 to $10 for men, but close kin who are able to do so and compadres are expected to contribute considerably more cash plus a certain amount of food and services. At all fiestas the public paying of cash contributions is one of the most important ritual acts. Men pay their contributions, called *cuotas*, at a table presided over by a president, secretary, and treasurer appointed for the occasion. The religious nature of this act is clear from the name given the men's table— santa mesa—which is the same term as that applied to the household shrine. The president greets each contributor formally, the secretary records his contribution, and the treasurer collects and guards the receipts. Another office is that of the toast pourer, a duty which may be shared by two or more men alternately. At the end of the santa mesa is a series of two or more long benches on which the men guests sit after paying their cuotas. The host sits at the head of these, next to the santa mesa, usually followed by his close kin and compadres. Each contribution initiates a round of mezcal toasts and cigarette smoking in honor of the contributor.

Women pay their contributions, called *limosna*, at the women's table which is not referred to as a santa mesa and may not be a table but a large basket or bowl placed on the floor or on a table, and is presided over by usually only one woman. Each woman receives a toast of sweet wine and a cigarette when she gives her limosna. She wears the cigarette behind her ear throughout the fiesta as a symbol of having paid her contribution. At some fiestas she also has the opportunity to buy a paper flower for an extra peso or two which she wears tucked in her hair behind her other ear. All invited women guests do not drink the wine toast at every contribution but are served perhaps two or three times during the course of the fiesta. Women drink beer more or less continuously during the fiesta, but this is not done ritually as with the wine.[7] Sometimes limosna is recorded but more frequently it is not.

It is not uncommon for a woman to make a contribution at the men's santa mesa for an absent or deceased husband. At such time the men toast the absent man with mezcal while the woman acting on his behalf is served the women's sweet wine. Observation at many fiestas of various types did not reveal any man making a contribution for a woman at the women's table. In cases known to me, a woman who was invited but unable to attend sent her contribution with a daughter before the event or with a friend or kinswoman who was also invited.

A couple attending a fiesta as invited guests must spend a minimum of $8, often considerably more, but it is not imperative for both to attend. The household's honor will be upheld equally whether one or both attend, the wife making a contribution for an absent husband and thus getting their name on the list of contributors. Women admitted that if they simply did not have the cash, they sometimes invented an excuse and "forgot" to send their contribution, but this

---

[7] Respectable Isthmus Zapotec women do not drink beer on other occasions and never drink mezcal or other strong alcoholic beverages.

Author's godchild wearing miniature fiesta costume.

was apparently done only in exceptional circumstances. If these lapses of memory were very frequent, gossip would probably result and the household's name would begin to appear less frequently among invited guests. At public fiestas and at weddings the total amounts of cuotas and of limosna are announced separately over the public address system at the end of the fiesta, followed by a round of applause.

Participation in Fiestas as Voluntary Contributor

The last category of participants in fiestas is that of voluntary contributor. These almost always outnumber invited guests at family fiestas. Any person, even a complete stranger, is welcome to enter a fiesta, make a contribution, receive his toast or gift and depart. If the donor is a man, he pays at the men's santa mesa, receives a cigarette and a toast of mezcal, and has his name entered in the ledger before he leaves. Because many more women and girls than men make voluntary contributions, there is often a special place set aside for them near the kitchen or back entrance. There two or three women will be in charge of accepting contributions and giving the contributor some food, typically a small clay bowl of *mole* with two or three warm tortillas placed on top. This is also given to invited women guests when they leave the fiesta. The usual voluntary contribution is $3 for women and $5 for men but sometimes several choices are offered to women, the amount of food given varying accordingly. In addition, special items are sometimes sold to pay certain costs. For example, at one mixa guétu I attended, women who contributed $3 received one *torta*, one chocolate tablet, and a small bowl of mole. For $5 they received two tortas, two chocolate tablets, and a slightly larger serving of mole. Sprigs of *cordoncillo* could be purchased separately for 50 centavos, the proceeds going to pay for grinding the maize for tortillas.

Households make great effort to contribute voluntarily to every fiesta in their neighborhood plus as many others as possible farther afield. Women make the greatest majority of voluntary contributions on behalf of their household, probably because the man of the house is occupied in his fields or at his trade unless he is an invited guest. If several fiestas happen to occur within a short time, voluntary contributions can strain the resources of a poor household severely. For whatever reason, it often happens that a particular household has no cash at all at the moment it is needed; for example, at the death of a neighbor. In such cases the woman of the household will use every resource she has to get the few pesos for the contribution. Perhaps she can sell a hen or a small piglet or pawn her earrings. Or she may have a sister or a *comadre* from whom she can borrow for a few days.

The reason ritual contributions are so important is not difficult to understand considering the facts of life and death in San Juan Evangelista. Every household must meet ritual expenses some time, often unexpectedly when resources are low. Very rarely is there any steady source of income such as wages or salary. The people respond to this "culture of insecurity" with their own mutual-aid mechanism in the form of cuotas and limosna. One household's ritual contribution to another will be reciprocated on a similar occasion later. Every ritual contribution, voluntary or otherwise, represents either the payment of ritual obligations or the prepayment toward ritual obligations the household anticipates at some future date, an on-going system in which a balance is never struck. But it is more than simple economic expediency which motivates people to make voluntary ritual contributions. Perhaps more importantly, contributions are a means of maintaining the household's status in the community. People who cooperate, who contribute as often as possible, even the poorest, will be spoken of as *buena gente* while households who refuse to participate or participate with reluctance will be ostracized. "*No corresponde*," Juanecos say of such persons. "When he dies, there will be no one to carry him to the cemetery." To Isthmus Zapotecs who value so highly the security of kinsmen and neighbors a worse fate would be difficult to imagine.

The proportion of expenses paid by contributions varies widely according to the type of fiesta and the status and resources of the sponsoring household. Records were obtained from several households which included all types of contributions from relatives, compadres, invited guests, and volunteer contributors. Contributions paid nearly 40 percent of the total expenses of a public fiesta, 35 percent of a mixa guétu, and 20 percent of a very elaborate wedding given by a wealthy household. One informant reported that contributions financed the entire burial and mixa guétu for her mother because, as she explained, "we have contributed to almost everyone in the pueblo at some time. Many people owed us."

OTHER RELIGIOUS EXPERIENCES

There exist, in addition to those involved in the fiesta system, many other possibilities for making and fulfilling vows to the saints. This is a characteristic of Latin American folk Catholicism and is not unique to San Juan Evangelista, yet it is so much a part of the everyday lives of people that the discussion of religion and ritual would not be complete without some reference to it. Zapotecs also often make vows to honor ancestors. For example, a friend vowed to honor her deceased mother by going to a church in another community every month for one year on the anniversary of her mother's death. Making and fulfilling small vows is so common that people rarely mention them. It is the rare, perhaps once in a lifetime, fulfillment of vows which informants recount with pride. Among these are pilgrimages to the shrine at Esquipulas, Guatemala, more than a thousand miles distant. Formerly it was undertaken on foot and horseback, all persons from the pueblo who vowed to go traveling together. The trip required almost three months and entailed great hardships and dangers. Older people recall how everyone left at home rejoiced when the pilgrims finally returned safely. Now the trip can be made by rail and bus in a week to ten days. Fewer persons go each year than formerly. Another popular pilgrimage is to Astata, only eight to ten hours by *redila* but still a hazardous journey because of primitive mountain roads. Astata is the site of miraculous rocks which are said to drip the blood of a saint and to produce water as long as a candle is kept burning in honor of the saint. Several informants had made this trip to fulfill vows, although a few women from El Centro go to sell at the fair rather than for religious purposes.

Another means of fulfilling vows involves building a chapel in honor of the saint. The several chapels which dot San Juan Evangelista all originated this way, the newest built at the entrance to the cemetery only a few years ago by a young matron, the nature of whose vow I neglected to learn. The construction of such a chapel in honor of a saint is considered a community service because it brings the saint's blessings to the whole community just as do celebrations in honor of the patron saints.

SUMMARY

In summing up the fiesta system as it exists today in San Juan Evangelista, it is apparent that sponsoring public fiestas is still an important means of gaining the highest respect of the community. Hosting private fiestas also adds to status and prestige, especially when food, drink, and music are abundantly supplied. Sponsoring baptisms and weddings is another status-enhancing activity. All these separate acts are cumulative in their effects on the household's status. Persons who are most frequently invited to fiestas are the gray-haired elders who have made countless ritual contributions, have sponsored baptisms and marriages, have hosted family fiestas, and perhaps have acted as mayordomos or anticipate doing so in the future. In effect, such persons have lived a life of service to their community for which they receive the honor and respect of their neighbors and status and prestige increasing through time. A household need not accumulate wealth to gain respect. The ideal rather is to share one's wealth for the benefit of the community, the ancestors, and the saints.

Anthropologists have often explained the widespread Latin American fiesta system as a leveling device, a way of insuring that community solidarity is not threatened by great differences in wealth. Development agencies have most often viewed the system as a block to capital accumulation and subsequent investment in capital-producing goods on which economic development depends. Both are correct when the system is viewed from afar. Yet it is important to remember that to the people within the system it is the social ties which the fiesta system establishes and maintains that give life meaning.

Nonetheless, indications are that in San Juan Evangelista as elsewhere the fiesta system is losing ground. It is deprecated by members of the mestizo culture as wasteful and senseless, views which are presented to school children. Men now rarely cooperate to provide the necessary labor of erecting the enramada, slaughtering the animals, and other heavy tasks of fiestas. This labor must be paid nowadays. The women continue their cooperative labor and their enthusiasm perhaps because for the women the fiesta system remains one of the most important aspects of life, almost the only diversion in a life of hard work and monotonous routine, something to look forward to in the later periods of life when the cumulative effects of participation in the system will have enhanced one's status and prestige. This is not to say that the fiesta system has lost its meaning for the men. They still participate along with the womenfolk on behalf of their households, although their cooperative labor has virtually disappeared. Still most of them, except the very old and the most traditional, seem less enthusiastic than are the women.

So the system will probably die in San Juan Evangelista as it has in so many other communities. Weddings, funerals, and mixa guétu will still occur but the reciprocal relations behind them which form the core of the social system will probably gradually decline, leaving a vacuum in the lives of the people which will be hard to fill, something I think will be especially tragic for the women.

7 / Social relations in
nonritual contexts

Conceptualizing the Isthmus Zapotec social system in terms of an overlay map, each successive layer of which represents a level of the social system, we have exposed and examined several layers of the social system in previous chapters. The preceding chapter described the prevalent behavior patterns and types of social relations associated with religious rituals. The present chapter is concerned with two overlays or levels simultaneously: social relations in secular contexts and the underlying beliefs and attitudes which form the bases of behavior in such non-religious contexts. It will be necessary to describe social relations first briefly, then go to the next level of underlying beliefs and attitudes—the ways people perceive their environment and the bases of such perceptions—and then return once again to social relations in nonreligious contexts.

We have learned in the previous chapter that the people of San Juan Evangelista come together in large groups in the fiesta system and cooperate to accomplish a particular goal, whether it be honoring the patron saint, celebrating a marriage, or paying homage to the dead. Particularly noteworthy is the fact that such large, cooperating, face-to-face groups organized for a common purpose occur almost wholly in religious contexts. Without the sanctions of religion the people seem unable or unwilling to cooperate in large face-to-face groups to accomplish some purpose. There are no voluntary associations such as economic cooperatives, unions, parent-teacher associations, fraternal orders, service clubs, and many others so familiar to North Americans. A few associations which exist of necessity "on paper" seldom if ever meet as a group. Suspicion and secrecy permeate secular social relations. Physical aggression and even violence are expected from neighbor and stranger alike; the universe is perceived as filled with threats and dangers. Fear, one discovers, is a dominant emotion in San Juan Evangelista. People *express* many specific fears—of strangers, of the unknown road, of wild creatures supposed to inhabit the mountains, of being alone, of illness, of ghosts, of envy and anger, of thieves and burglars, of bats, and witches.[1] The list is far too lengthy to sum-

---

[1] I had a quite undeserved reputation for valor which rested mainly on the fact that I had driven a pickup truck all the way from the United States to San Juan Evangelista alone and that I lived alone during the first ten months of fieldwork. As to living alone, what people mistook for courage was actually more the result of circumstances and an inadequate understanding of the culture. I would not repeat that mistake.

marize here. An equally long list of unexpressed fears manifest themselves in people's behavior—fear of conflict, of political involvement, of falling victim to the perfidy of a friend, of betrayal of a confidence, for example.

Clearly, the people of San Juan Evangelista view their environment, indeed their whole universe, as essentially threatening and dangerous. Why? In terms of Isthmus Zapotec peasant culture, I think their view of the universe is not unrealistic. Given the general state of insecurity and the more or less continuous threat of real disaster which hovers over people's lives in the form of destitution, illness, and death, people's fears simply express their anxieties over the uncertainties which face them daily. Add to these real threats the body of beliefs and attitudes concerning causes of illness, death, and other misfortunes and something which might be called a "culture of insecurity" emerges.[2] Behavior, which at first seems irrational, even paranoid, to the outsider, begins to make sense in the context of the Isthmus Zapotec social system.

Of course people in every society face some degree of uncertainty in life. In peasant communities generally as in San Juan Evangelista, the level of insecurity is many times greater than it is in our own society because people live much closer to an absolute subsistence level than most of us can imagine. In such a community what would be a small adversity for ourselves can be a disaster. Because of a general low level of health and sanitation, illness can be very serious, frequently fatal. One's land and possessions can disappear through treachery, legal maneuvers, and thievery, one's assets can be quickly dissipated in medicine, drugs, medical doctor's fees, and the more modest fees of native curers. Insecurity, then, centers around loss of health, life, and property. The causes as well as the agents of misfortune may be natural or supernatural. For example, the arousal of envy in a neighbor can bring misfortune and disaster to a household in various forms. The envious person may injure through actual physical aggression, or he may work through supernatural means such as witchcraft and spell-casting. The prudent individual protects himself and his household from envy and other threats to security in many ways. First, he tries to avoid arousing envy by his own actions and behavior. Second, he tries to protect and fortify his household in order to limit the danger of physical aggression. Third, he protects himself and his household by supernatural means through the use of protective and preventive magic.

BEHAVIOR TO AVOID AROUSING ENVY

The wise person avoids arousing envy by taking certain precautions. He conceals possessions from the eyes of outsiders, neighbor and stranger alike. The mother covers the baby from harmful admiring glances, some of which may be open

---

[2] Foster (1965) explains many similar behavioral characteristics in Tzintzuntzan and other peasant communities as responses to a particular cognitive orientation which he terms "The Image of Limited Good." Foster's model fits the Isthmus Zapotec data well and could be used. However, the real threats and the perceived threats in San Juan Evangelista seem to me to be both adequate and more directly explanatory of behavior in the specific context of Isthmus Zapotec culture.

expressions of envy.[3] Gifts and purchases other than food are transported in covered receptacles or otherwise hidden from curious, perhaps envious, eyes. Any accumulation of goods or improvement in the household's circumstances is kept secret as long as possible. One cannot live long beside the main entrance to the pueblo without becoming aware of a considerable traffic by foot, by oxcart, by truck and taxicab, entering and leaving San Juan in the hours between midnight and dawn. At first I assumed that people wished to take advantage of the cooler temperature to move goods, begin long journeys, or begin preparations for early market transactions. All of these reasons are valid on some occasions, but a major reason, secrecy, escaped my attention for months. Only when I was making arrangements to move from the rented house into Doña Rufina's solar did the importance of secrecy become apparent.

Doña Rufina had been in my house many times and knew approximately the extent of my possessions. The furniture consisted mainly of shelving for books and storage and two work tables made locally of rough unfinished lumber, a portable typewriter, tape recorder, an old card table and a couple of ragged and rusty canvas lawn chairs. The paucity and humbleness of my possessions by North American standards was such that I had considered myself to be living very simply with the barest essentials. The heaviest moving task involved a dozen or so cartons of books, field notes, office supplies and papers. I did not anticipate that the move would require more than hiring a couple of *cargadores* for perhaps two hours. I asked Doña Rufina what would be a convenient time for moving. "Well, I've been thinking about that," she replied. "I think you should just bring one thing over here each night after dark. No one will realize you are moving all your things in here." I protested that the move would take too long. "But if people see you bringing all those things into my solar they are going to be envious of me," she said. I argued that everyone knew the furnishings were mine, not hers, so there would be no reason for people to envy her. But Doña Rufina was not convinced. "Take my advice. I have lived in this solar so many years [nearly forty] without trouble because I have always been cautious. ¡Fíjate! All those years I sold maize from my solar nobody knew how much I sold because I always had the *carretas* [of maize] delivered at night. When we built this house, I accumulated the *ladrillos* cartload by cartload for years, and nobody knew what we were about because everything was brought in at night. I kept the building supplies hidden over in that corner beyond the big rock until we had almost enough to complete the house." But in the end, after considerable discussion, Doña Rufina agreed that I might move in over the course of three or four evenings without arousing too much attention.

The examples cited by Doña Rufina are some of the kinds of precautions people take to avoid envy. There are many others. If one wishes to accomplish something or make a purchase which can be expected to arouse envy, a great deal of advance planning, maneuvering, and consideration of possible alternatives may be involved.

---

[3] There are other reasons for shielding the baby. In addition to envy, ojo may result from even a person of goodwill if they do not counteract the admiration with a pat on the head or buttocks of the child. Susto can also result from the baby being frightened by unfamiliar persons or objects.

In one case an informant wanted to buy *cebu* cattle as a investment. Government agencies have tried to encourage the breeding of these animals in preference to the criollos, but in San Juan Evangelista cebus are still uncommon, partly because they are costly animals. My informant, Jorge, considered the alternate plans of buying the herd one animal at a time over a period of months, of buying the whole herd of twelve animals at one time and donating two of them to the saint's herd to "show people I am *buena gente*," and of buying only six young calves at first "to see what happens." In the course of six or seven months during which Jorge considered the best approach, there were probably other possible courses of action considered and forgotten by Jorge during the intervals between our occasional conversations. Finally Jorge purchased two cebu calves and used the rest of his savings to buy a herd of criollos from a relative because in this way nobody would realize that the criollos had changed owners and the two small cebus would be scarcely noticed.[4]

SECURING THE SOLAR

One of the best protections against acts of physical aggression, whatever the cause, is a secure solar. In San Juan Evangelista the more prosperous the household, the more secure will be the solar for two reasons. Making a solar impervious to intruders is costly, and the prosperous household provides the most tempting target to would-be thieves as well as being most vulnerable to envy. A secure solar is enclosed on all sides by an 8- to 10-foot-high adobe wall, often topped with jagged broken glass. There is a single opening to the street which can be securely barred. In modern solares, the door may be metal instead of wood. A secure solar in San Juan Evangelista probably will not have a window, but if it does, the window opening will be covered with iron grillwork and closable from the inside by wooden shutters. Glass windowpanes are avoided since they present an irresistible temptation to rock-wielders. If there is a window which opens onto the street, one must be careful not to sleep or place a sleeping child near an unshuttered window even in the daytime. It is too easy for any passerby to toss a rock or bottle through the opening. Also precautions must be taken to keep objects inside the room far enough from the window so that they cannot be reached by long arms of passersby. All possessions, including maize, mangoes, coconuts, bananas, or other products brought in from the fields must be stored within the solar. The only animals more or less immune to theft are pigs, dogs, and cats. Cattle thefts in el monte occur with such regularity that people view the losses as calculated risks of owning cattle. Even growing crops are not safe from thieves and vandalism.[5] Physical aggression, which may be caused by envy or anger or simply because the victim offers an easy target, is usually attributed to males and seems most often to be directed toward other males, in part because the

---

[4] Cattle are pastured on communal lands. In this case the purchased herd remained in the same area it had been previously, only the owner and the caretaker changing.

[5] Celso found several rows of a small patch of sorgo cut and removed by thieves shortly before it was ready for harvest. This field was about four miles from the pueblo.

socialization process of girls includes actions and behavior designed to avoid and discourage male aggression. Not infrequently physical aggression expresses itself in homicide, which may spark a series of reprisals.

Supernaturally caused misfortunes are especially feared because the agent which brings them may be as elusive as a will-o'-the-wisp, and cure is impossible until the agent is identified. Therefore, a household can be rapidly impoverished to the point of destitution while seeking the causes and trying various cures for a series of misfortunes or a lingering illness. Again prevention through one's own actions is the wisest procedure. Supernatural causes are only discovered *post facto*. That is to say some misfortune, usually illness, occurs. It does not respond to the usual simple treatments of curanderas, medicines, perhaps efforts of a medical doctor, and certainly nowadays injections of antibiotics. The first curandera called will have divined a cause before treatment and acted accordingly. Probably other curers will be called in succession, each of whom will divine a cause and treat the patient for a time. This can continue until the patient is cured or the family's patience or resources are exhausted. Witchcraft may be cured by stronger counter-magic. The diviner cautions the client not to reveal the identity of the witch lest she (or he) invoke more powerful magic against the victim. Other supernatural agents include spirits of the dead. One who dies violently may linger around the cemetery for years, frightening passersby, pursuing them through the streets at night, and playing the usual ghostly tricks. Quarrels and conflicts between persons might cause the spirit of the one who first dies to plague the other. The best protection is to be especially careful to observe all the death rituals with proper respect so that the spirit will be content to forget the earlier conflict. Even though there has been no conflict, deceased kin can cause trouble for the living. Perhaps a promesa was left unfulfilled or the spirit may simply be reluctant to leave his home and his loved ones. Who knows what spirits of the dead may do? Again, proper attention to death rituals is the best insurance against later complications.

But if supernatural causes are only discovered after the fact, the threat is constantly present. Any unfamiliar person who behaves suspiciously, an animal which acts strangely, and even an unfamiliar discarded object tossed carelessly in front of one's door are causes for alarm.[6] Again preventive measures and precautions are wise. The curandera is called when there is a possibility that one has been exposed to supernatural forces.

Women are thought to be witches more often than are men, perhaps because witches are also usually curers and there are many more curanderas than curanderos. Women also employ native curers for themselves and their children many times more frequently than in the case of adult men. As an informant stated, "We [women] use curanderas so much because we have so much trouble [illness]." Contrary to reports from some other peasant communities in Mesoamerica, the

---

[6] During mango season when I was selling mangoes with my informants in the Oaxaca market place, a mestizo woman loitered around among the vendors most of one day trying to entice young women to "go to work for me in Mexico," offering to pay $1,000 per month. The work was supposed to be care for an invalid son, but by her actions I guessed she might be connected with some illegal activity such as prostitution. The girls, however, avoided her because her behavior indicated to them that she was a witch.

witch may be a close neighbor to the victim.[7] Conflicts are avoided between the victim and the witch because the latter's identity must remain a closely guarded secret between the diviner and the victim. But even if one's neighbor is not known to be a witch, a chance remark overheard can be interpreted as an evil wish. For example, an informant's twelve-year-old son became ill and remained so despite every effort to cure him including consulting medical doctors who diagnosed the trouble as a kidney ailment. After several months the boy's condition seemed actually to be deteriorating. One day the mother overheard her neighbor remark to a visitor that it appeared the boy might die. The mother was deeply disturbed, interpreting the neighbor's remark as a wish that the boy would die. She immediately began to think of her neighbor as the possible cause of the boy's illness, although of course this was not revealed to the neighbor.

One's own strong emotions can also be dangerous. A person can die from his own anger, and suppressed anger can be as lethal as anger expressed. It is easy to understand why people fear situations in which differences of opinion and conflicts might arise. Illness and death caused by anger arising within the victim is referred to as *coraje* just as illness caused by fright is referred to as *susto* or *espanto*.[8] One avoids frightening or startling another person. Even a small child in San Juan Evangelista knows better than to sneak up behind his friend and cover the other's eyes with his hands. That would be an intentional attempt to cause susto. To avoid sudden fright, people try to make their presence known when one's back is turned or something prevents one from hearing another's approach. On one occasion I was startled by my closest friend while typing. She was so upset that she almost wept for fear she had given me susto, explaining that she had called and thought I had answered.

Admiring glances directed toward women and children, whether or not the admirer's intentions are friendly, can give rise to illness. The admirer may be of either sex but the admired are almost always women and children because "we are more attractive and others are jealous," an informant explained. Therefore, children are kept in the solar out of sight of admiring glances.[9] People who "know how to act" may admire the baby openly because they counteract any possible harm from ojo by patting the child's head or buttocks. Attractive women may have trouble all their lives which require the frequent employment of curanderas to counteract ojo.

---

[7] In some Mesoamerican peasant communities witches are reported to always be identified as someone living at the opposite end of the pueblo. Such identification may serve the same purpose as keeping the witch's identity secret in San Juan Evangelista—that is, to avoid open accusations and overt hostility. One of my informants in San Juan was employing a curer in 1967 who had been identified as responsible for some family illness several years previously. The illness was later found to be caused by the spirit of the deceased household head, after which it was cured. Of course, the curandera was not aware that she had been accused of witchcraft previously.

[8] In some places, susto and espanto are distinguished. Susto is usually an illness which is caused by a real fright while espanto is an illness caused by some supernatural agent. In San Juan Evangelista the two are used interchangeably for either.

[9] Doña Rufina related of her second daughter: "Amalia was such a beautiful child with her curly hair that we were always having to call the curer for her. Even now that she is many years married and with children she still has trouble."

A healthy person is better able to ward off illness whatever the cause, and people clearly understand that a weak body will be more susceptible to serious illness. There is great concern with health and the maintenance of a healthy body, although the preventive and precautionary practices are not the same as those prescribed by modern medicine. One protects his health by trying to maintain a balance between the effects of hot and cold on the body's humors, a concept that derives from Hippocratic medicine via sixteenth-century Spain and is widespread still in Latin America. If a person has a fever he does not aggravate it by eating or drinking hot substances. One protects himself from the night's chill by not eating or drinking cold substances in the late afternoon.[10] Most fruits are considered cold and avoided in the *tardecita* as are other cold foods.

It is not possible in this brief case study to describe in all its rich detail the many threats to health, life, and property and the attendant behavior which is so much a part of day-to-day living in San Juan Evangelista. Adequate treatment of just this single aspect of Isthmus Zapotec culture would require a volume much longer than the present one. I have tried to convey to the reader something of the beliefs and attitudes which strongly influence people's behavior, and to illustrate that in terms of the beliefs and the conditions of life, the Isthmus Zapotec world *is* a dangerous and threatening place. It must be stressed that the residents of San Juan Evangelista are not unique. They share their beliefs and behavior with all Isthmus Zapotecs of similar socioeconomic conditions and to a large extent with all peasant peoples of Mesoamerica. Some traits described here have a much wider distribution in peasant communities and many are not confined to Mesoamerica. Nor would it be fair to neglect to mention that some residents of San Juan Evangelista consider these folk beliefs as superstitions and that many elites in El Centro, not native to the Isthmus, believe in and practice some of this "folk medicine," even though they say it is all superstition only believed by poor, ignorant campesinos. Indeed, I think it would be difficult to live in the Isthmus for any length of time *without* coming to practice and even believe in the efficacy of the folk medicine, *without* becoming suspicious, distrustful, and secretive.

There is some evidence, not substantiated by research, that the Isthmus of Tehuantepec may be the scene of more political unrest and physical aggression than is generally true of Mesoamerica. Again, two conditions may exist in San Juan Evangelista itself which could enhance the anxiety level. The first concerns land and municipio boundaries about which the people surely have good reason to feel insecure and threatened. (See Chap. 4.) The second condition, for which I lack comparative data from other Isthmus communities, is the relatively high level of physical aggression and violence. Some of this aggression occurs between residents of the pueblo to be sure, but a considerable amount of such behavior seems to be directed toward Juanecos by individuals and factions outside the municipio. Whatever the rationalization of Istmeños, I suspect that the old political factionalism continues to be a strong incentive to aggressive acts. San Juan Evangelista's

---

[10] The identity of a substance as hot or cold is not logical in our terms. Ice, for example, is a "hot" substance. Those foods identified as either hot or cold vary somewhat between informants in San Juan Evangelista and also there is variation between San Juan Evangelista and other parts of Mesoamerica.

location combined with inadequate and almost totally ineffective law enforcement makes the muncipio and the pueblo an ideal haven for criminal elements. In addition, the pueblo may attract acts of vandalism by outsiders simply because the chances of apprehension are so small.[11] These conditions could lead the residents of San Juan to feel more vulnerable and insecure than is true for el Istmo in general. While certain groups and individuals in El Centro characterize the people of San Juan Evangelista as especially aggressive, violent, and barbarian, my research and impressions cannot support such an opinion. Acts of physical aggression and violence occur in every Isthmus community and indeed in every human community.

SOCIAL RELATIONS IN AN INSECURE ENVIRONMENT

In the first part of the chapter the focus has been on the people's perception of their environment as dangerous and threatening and the precautionary measures which are taken to ward off or reduce the dangers. In this section, social relations are described beginning with the household, then progressing to the larger kin group, compadrazgo, neighborhood, and the community at large.

Social Relations within the Household

The household is the basic social as well as economic unit, its members closely bound together by ties of kinship, affection, and mutual dependence. The household is the most closely knit group in Isthmus Zapotec culture, although the members are not given to open displays of affection except toward babies and toddlers. As in all human families, sex and relative age are major determinants of roles within the household. The eldest able-bodied couple are the acknowledged heads, the man being the official representative of the household in affairs of the community at large, but the wife representing the household in contacts with other women. Ideally, the male elder member of the household is "head of the household." In practice, the husband-wife team forms a strong, egalitarian partnership with much of the actual burden of day-to-day responsibility and decision-making falling on the wife. Since she has been well prepared by a long apprenticeship first in her mother's household and later in that of her mother-in-law, when she at last heads her own household, it is most often with confidence and efficiency borne of experience and maturity. Dependent, clinging-vine-type wives are so rare in San Juan Evangelista that I met none at all in interviewing more than fifty wives in a household survey.

An essential function of the Isthmus Zapotec household is mutual protection. The male role centers around actual physical protection while female roles are

---

[11] This seems to have been true in my case. Several attacks of rock throwing during the night hours culminated in two young men gaining sufficient courage to climb through the window into my sleeping quarters. Fortunately I awoke and fled. Although I was the target, the cause was probably nothing more than the fact that I was a woman living alone in a house that did not offer sufficient protection. The aggressors in this case were almost certainly not residents of San Juan Evangelista.

more concerned with protecting the health of the household members through proper preventive and curative measures. Previously it was noted that Zapotecs do not enjoy solitude and never live alone by preference. The more household members, the more secure is the household from physical acts of aggression. A person left alone by death or circumstances can usually "borrow" nieces, nephews, grandchildren, or more distant young relatives to live in the solar, or close the solar and move into the home of kin. The household without an adult male in residence is in a more vulnerable position than would otherwise be the case. Nonetheless, circumstances often force elderly sisters or a mother and daughter to live alone.

Doña Rufina related that when she and her twelve-year-old daughter lived alone in the solar for some months after her husband's death, they were so frightened that they huddled together at night in a single hammock, trembling at every unfamiliar sound. Most of the solar was secured by metal doors with locks but the back part where the cooking was done had only a reed fence. Doña Rufina painted a broad white stripe on the house wall there where it would be visible to an intruder. She thought the stripe would frighten an intruder who would mistake it for a man in the dark. The stripe was still doing sentry duty ten years later during my residence in the solar. A few months after Doña Rufina's husband died, her youngest daughter fell ill. In the process of discovering the cause of the illness and trying various cures, Doña Rufina had the solar cured, and thereafter she felt more secure.[12]

As noted earlier, the poorer the household the less secure it will be because locks, iron grillwork, and metal doors, as well as high adobe walls, are costly. On the other hand, the poor household does not feel as threatened in terms of thieves, burglars, and other acts of physical aggression because of its poverty. "Who would be so foolish as to think we had anything worth stealing?" or "We are just poor simple people with nothing to fear," the people say, but this is only relatively true. An informant, Rosita, and her husband lived in a very small solar without modern conveniences. The floor of the little house was of packed earth, the two window openings had been filled with loose adobes against a time when they might be able to install grillwork and shutters, the solar was enclosed with only a reed fence and closed with a rickety reed gate that had to be propped shut with a pole. Usually this childless couple felt moderately secure from intruders because they had nothing of value in the solar, but when they temporarily had to store maize, sesame, or mangoes after harvest one of them had to remain in the solar at all times until the produce was sold and delivered. "If I am not right here," said Rosita, "the *mazorca* will just 'walk away.'"

The household, then, offers physical security from outside threats as well as emotional and economic security to its members. Anyone who lives alone by

---

[12] Curing a solar involves hiring a curandero who comes at midnight and places magical substances including a pair of *chiles anchos* in previously prepared holes in the floor and walls of the solar, the latter near entrances and openings. During this process, the curandero is chanting prayers. The holes are then sealed over so that they cannot be easily detected. Curing a solar is a closely guarded secret because the protection is only effective if nobody outside the household has knowledge of it.

preference, as I did for a time, is completely beyond comprehension; a person without kin is to be pitied. When I was introduced to someone for the first time it was always with the explanation that "she is all alone, far from her family."

Social Relations with Kin outside the Household

The bilateral kinship system and prevalence of community endogamy (that is, most marriage partners are natives of San Juan) mean that a great many households in the community are related by kinship and marriage to a number of others. But the pattern of emigration, which is of long standing, and patrilocal residence also have the effect of widening the kinship circle to include families in distant places, especially the national capital and the state of Veracruz. The kindred, that group of persons which each individual recognizes as his kin, never functions as a unit, although portions of the group cooperate on ritual occasions. In day-to-day living, kin ties outside the household may, but do not necessarily, take precedence over those with nonkin. Most persons are on friendly terms with part of their kindred, indifferent or even hostile to others. The Isthmus Zapotec ideal is that social relations between siblings will always be close and cordial throughout life, and that kinship itself, whatever the degree, should always manifest itself in mutual trust and cooperation. Those ideals are seldom realized.

After siblings reach adulthood and marry, close relations between them may continue or may cool to the point of noncommunication. Conflicts among adult siblings often seem to arise over matters of inheritance. Among the five separate families of adult siblings with which I was most familiar, only one, which consisted of three sisters, was not divided. In three of the other four families, conflicts and alienation were of long duration. In the fourth, the disagreements were recent and may since have been resolved. Adult children may even quarrel with their aged parents over favoritism shown to siblings, although respect for parents seems usually to prevent complete alienation. Nonetheless, adult siblings who remain on friendly terms provide mutual assistance and protection to one another beyond what can be expected of any other kin outside the household, and it remains probably the closest relationship beyond the household unit.

Social Relations with Compadres

The compadre relationship, as we have noted previously, is primarily a formal one. It is very important also in terms of mutual security, providing a relationship *de confianza* second only to real kin.[13] Once established, the compadre relationship ideally remains active throughout the lives of the persons involved, binding the households of compadres into a reciprocal supportive relationship resembling that of true kin. Compadres owe one another moral and financial support in times of

[13] Berta, a middle-aged widow, was comadre to Rosalia by virtue of having sponsored Rosalia's daughter at baptism. When the child was about six years old, Berta became her aunt as well as her *madrina* by marrying Rosalia's brother. There was some discussion between the former comadres, now sisters-in-law, about whether the little girl should continue referring to Berta as madrina or should begin calling her *tia*. The mother, Rosalia, suggested that tia was more appropriate because the kin relationship [even though affinal rather than biological in this case] was closer and more intimate than that between fictive kin.

crises and on ritual occasions. Padrinos (referring to couples) are usually called in to arbitrate marital problems or family conflicts among adult siblings after parents die. However, the nature of Isthmus Zapotec social relations is such that many compadre relations also break down. Sometimes there is a complete break and the two couples involved simply cease to recognize the existence of the relationship. More often the relationship gradually becomes inactive over time unless it is reaffirmed at frequent intervals through reciprocal behavior—courtesies, gifts, invitations, and such. In other words, to remain effective the compadre relationship is one in which both couples must consciously work to reaffirm it through reciprocal acts. This is easier when both couples live in the same community and are more or less social equals. Perhaps this is the main reason the people of San Juan Evangelista prefer to establish compadre relationships within their own community and social class. The few compadre relationships established outside tend to be mainly inactive unless there is frequent contact, such as between women vendors occupying adjacent stalls in the market place.

Social Relations among Neighbors

The people of San Juan Evangelista seem very urbanized in their attitude toward nonkin neighbors in that they prefer to keep a certain degree of social distance while remaining on neighborly terms. Because adjoining solares often have only reed walls separating them (although the ideal is adobe), privacy between neighbors can be a problem in small solares. Mainly neighbors support one another in ritual contributions, especially those involving deaths. Women neighbors seem to cooperate in small, informal ways more than men but that may be simply because women have more need to exchange services and spend more time in relatively close contact in the neighborhood than do men. Certainly it would be much more difficult for a woman to live on unfriendly terms with her neighbors than it would be for her husband who is usually away during the day.

Among neighbors, then, there is little intimacy or genuine supportive friendship unless kinship is also involved, but one can usually count on neighbors for help in times of mutual threat—for example, to chase away intruders or to protect the solares from threats of fire, floods, and other natural disasters—on ritual occasions, and in mutually beneficial economic transactions.

Social Relations in the Community

In the first pages of this chapter, the absence of secular voluntary associations was noted. The people of San Juan Evangelista, therefore, do not meet in groups to make community decisions. This is especially apparent when one discovers that those organizations or associations which do exist on paper by virtue of necessity seldom if ever meet as a group.[14] Instead, the group's business is conducted on a dyadic basis. Indeed, one of the most striking aspects of Isthmus Zapotec social structure, when compared to our own, is the very strong preference for dyadic

---

[14] An example is the association of *ganaderos* to which every cattle owner belongs because he owns cattle. No cattle can change ownership without a certification of ownership by the seller through this association.

relationships, those involving only two persons or couples.[15] This means that if a group decision must be reached or a certain amount of consensus ascertained, concerned individuals will discuss the matter privately on a dyadic basis with those other members with which they have amicable relationships. This amounts to sort of an informal poll-taking to assess support or opposition by the few individuals most interested in the subject at hand. Action will finally be taken along the lines indicated by the majority of the members unless the dissenting minority has rather pronounced objections, in which case a split into strongly antagonistic opposing factions may occur, thus preventing the taking of any constructive action whatever.

Since organized opposition can paralyze decision-making, very commonly individuals in charge try to make unilateral decisions covertly. These often lead to *post facto* conflicts, of course, but the more unilateral decisions that can be made and the fewer of these which become public knowledge, the better the chance of some action being taken on behalf of the group, whether or not it is the best or preferred action of the group as a whole.

When leadership is in doubt, that part of the community which might reasonably be counted on for support can be polled on a dyadic basis, while those individuals who might be expected to oppose the decision or action may be "inadvertently" bypassed. During 1966–1967 there was some effort to crystallize opinions by circulating petitions which household heads were asked to sign if they favored the proposed action. As a hypothetical example, suppose that an individual was dissatisfied with certain actions or inactions of the pueblo's *presidente*. The dissatisfied individual could circulate a petition stating his case and asking for signatures of persons in favor of relieving the presidente of his office. Naturally the complainant would contact first those households where he could count on support, while trying to muster as many signatures as possible before the presidente and his friends learned of the plan. The presidente's supporters would probably begin circulating a counter petition as soon as they received news of the first. Eventually each side would have a petition with the signatures of those household heads on which they could count for support. How successful the circulating of petitions has been is uncertain. A number of informants claimed they never signed petitions because it was too easy to become embroiled in controversy. There is a feeling that committing oneself to any side of a conflict is dangerous and can lead to disastrous consequences. Signing a petition commits the signer unequivocally, whereas verbal commitments can be more easily evaded and denied. Perhaps indicative of people's attitude toward petitions was the story making the rounds, probably untrue, of the local *politico* who was embarrassed to discover he had signed petitions of two opposing factions.

It is apparent that community action outside the context of religion is very difficult to achieve. Perhaps this is one of the reasons that the cargo system evolved in the colonial period through which local political and religious offices and duties

---

[15] The preference for dyadic relationships is widespread in Mesoamerican peasant communities as well as in other areas of the world. See especially Foster 1961, "The Dyadic Contract: A Model for the Social Structure of a Mexican Peasant Village." Foster's model and features of it have been employed by a number of anthropologists since 1961.

were bound together. In San Juan Evangelista, at any rate, the absence of religious sanctions in community affairs effectively forestalls cooperation and community decision-making and leads people to distrust local leadership and one another.

SUMMARY

While household ties are the closest, followed by close kin outside the household, then compadres, none of these relationships seems to be as close and binding in real life as the cultural ideals prescribe. Isthmus Zapotecs tend to be lonely individuals, even within the household unit, never completely trusting even the most trusted of kin. They seem to be continually searching for social relationships in which they can place trust and continually anticipating disappointment. Kin become alienated; compadres do not respond when such is their obligation; neighbors are spiteful and envious instead of friendly and cooperative as they should be. Every social relationship seems to be less enduring and less intimate than is desired. The individual longs for loyalty, friendship, and security, yet expects to be betrayed. People speak of being *celoso* not in terms of sexual jealousy but in terms of friendship and loyalty. Velia tells her comadre she is jealous because she saw her comadre talking to another woman. She expects an explanation and a reaffirmation of the comadre relationship. "Ay, comadre, it was nothing. She is only an acquaintance, a friend of my sister. She cannot take the place of my comadre," Velia's comadre reassures, but Velia is not completely convinced.

An atmosphere of real insecurity thus leads the people of San Juan Evangelista to feel threatened by real and imagined dangers. Insecurity feeds back upon itself, creating more and more protective, distrustful, suspicious behavior, until the entire social system is permeated with anxiety and paranoia. Cooperation in ritual contexts thus becomes important as a reaffirmation of faith in one's fellows and in social relations generally.

8 / Women and men: women's roles

In an attempt to explain that elusive quality of relationship between the sexes which has led casual observers to characterize the Isthmus Zapotec social system as a matriarchate, I now turn to the final stratum of the social overlay map.[1] At the beginning of the case study, I stated that Isthmus Zapotec society is very definitely not matriarchal. The picture I have drawn in subsequent chapters could more accurately be described as a patriarchate. But neither of these extremes is true. Isthmus Zapotec society in fact is a blend of roles which leads to a fine balance of equality between the sexes. As an explanatory device, the simple role model introduced in the first pages and more fully described below provides a framework for the incorporation of the case material presented in the last half of the chapter.

A ROLE MODEL

If one conceptualizes the social system as made up of roles (defined earlier as bundles of rights and obligations), one might compare a social system to an iceberg. What has been described to this point is the visible part of the iceberg, that part which includes the formalized roles. A large part of the Isthmus Zapotec social system, however, is concealed in the submerged part of the iceberg. The submerged part of the social system, the nonformalized roles, is as crucial to an understanding of Isthmus Zapotec culture as is the visible part, the formalized roles. Furthermore, it is in this submerged part of the system that the roles of women are so important.

Formalized and Nonformalized Roles

Formalized roles are here defined as those given formal status and recognition by the members of the society. That is to say, every adult member of the society recognizes the existence of the role and has a fairly clear concept of the rights and

---

[1] Anthropologists agree that matriarchies (that is, societies in which women rather than men exercise power in the public domain) do not exist and in all probability have never existed despite some enchanting myths, early travelers' reports, and nineteenth-century social evolutionary theories.

duties the role demands, even though he may never be expected to fill the role. Examples might be the role of mother, father, or presidente of the municipio. Nonformalized roles are those which are not so clearly perceived or rigidly defined by the members of the society. Most people may not be aware that the role exists, and even persons filling such nonformalized roles may perceive their own behavior as individual action without structure or pattern in the larger system. Only the observer becomes aware eventually that nonformalized roles exist, an awareness occasioned by observing repeated instances of similar behavior by many different individuals in many different contexts. A number of examples of nonformalized roles will be presented in the final pages of the chapter.

Anthropologists and sociologists, I believe, are uncomfortable with nonformalized roles even when they are well aware of their existence. The reason for this discomfort probably lies in the lack of effective research tools for investigating such roles systematically and the absence of models for integrating them into the ultimate description. Generally anthropologists have described the visible roles—that is, the formalized roles—since these are most readily observable and amenable to analysis and description. If the nonformalized roles are powerful, there has probably been some attempt to incorporate these into the description, often in an unsystematic way just as they occur in the field notes, leaving the reader to draw his own conclusions as to how to integrate them into the social system. Some attempts have been made to explain nonformalized roles by presenting the formalized roles as the social system and then adding data concerning nonformalized roles as "exceptions to the rules." A few more sophisticated attempts to deal with nonformalized roles will receive fuller treatment in following pages.

Public and Private Domains

A role model of Isthmus Zapotec society is represented in Fig. 8-1, with roles divided along a horizontal plane into formalized and nonformalized categories and along a vertical plane as existing in private or public domain. The private domain refers to the family or domestic group, while the public domain refers to the remainder of the social system. The rectangle in Fig. 8-1 represents the totality of roles which make up the social system, with Line A separating formalized and nonformalized roles and Line B separating private and public domains. The level of Line A is arbitrarily drawn to the degree that incomplete and inferential data indicate that nonformalized roles probably predominate in the Isthmus Zapotec social system. They may be more or less important than Line A indicates. On the basis of the wide range of variability known to exist in other aspects of social systems crossculturally, I would hypothesize that Line A might be drawn either considerably higher or considerably lower for any other specific social system.

The Sexes and Role Type

Although we can only guess at the adaptive significance of assignment of certain roles by sex or the evolutionary processes involved in such assignment, a universal fact of human society is that men fill most of the formalized roles in the public domain. Furthermore, in many societies, perhaps in most, men fill

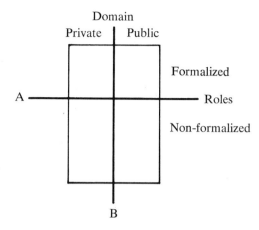

Fig. 8-1. Role model, San Juan Evangelista social system.

those formalized roles in the private domain which require regular interaction with male roles in the public domain. An example is the role of father as head of the family which will normally include his acting as intermediary between the family (private domain) and the outside world (public domain), especially but not exclusively where the role in the public domain is held by a man. This function of the male head of the family is very apparent in San Juan Evangelista, and it is quite evident even in our own social system.

Some roles in the public domain form complementary pairs by sex. An example would be the President and First Lady of the United States or the fiesta sponsor and his wife in San Juan Evangelista. However, complementary pairs seem to be few in the public domain in most social systems. In the private domain, on the other hand, they abound. Mother-father, husband-wife, brother-sister are all complementary pairs of roles as is that of parent-child, although the latter is assigned on the basis of relative age rather than sex.

Universal Role Assignment by Sex

In every society, women's formalized roles in the private domain include the major responsibility for rearing children in the early years of life. Nearly universally, the role of woman includes preparation of food for male adult members of the family as well as for children and the majority of domestic tasks in and near the house site.[2] As previously stated, among the domestic roles of men are those which require interaction or possible contact with persons filling formalized roles in the public domain. In addition, men's roles in the private domain center around making and maintaining the technology required for the man's subsistence activities and maintenance of order within and protection of the private domain.

Harris, in a recently published introductory textbook, summarizes universal roles assigned by sex as follows (1971:581–582):

[2] See Brown 1970.

1. In all hunting and gathering societies men specialize in hunting the large, dangerous, migratory, and swift game, while women specialize in small game, shellfish, and vegetable products.

2. In all known human societies men have exercised a dominant role in the maintenance of law and order in nondomestic contexts, especially in intergroup relations. (Matriarchy has never existed.)

3. In all known societies, the primary police-military force consists of males specially trained to use fighting weapons. Females are seldom trained to use such weapons.

4. In all societies, women are the specialists in rearing infants.

Roles and the "Status of Women"

In every human society status is assigned to formalized roles. Status is that degree of value or prestige which the society attaches to a particular role as compared to other roles. As a rule formalized roles in the public domain seem to be universally more important in conferring status than those in the private domain. There is no doubt that nonformalized roles may also confer status and prestige in some cases, as seems to be true for the Isthmus Zapotecs, but it is a difficult task to evaluate nonformalized roles along these lines because of their nature.

It is a truism that the "status of women" in any given society is never higher than that of the men; that is, women as a group are never accorded dominance over men as a group (Harris' No. 2 above). Where formalized roles occur in complementary pairs by sex, the male role of the pair is normally accorded higher status than the female role. The reasons for such regularities having developed and philosophical arguments about their justification, although intriguing subjects, are beyond the scope of this case study. The higher value placed on men's roles is not necessarily derived from rational considerations. For example, in hunting and gathering societies men's subsistence activities are always the most prestigious, yet women's subsistence activities almost always contribute considerably more than 50 percent of the total food supply of the group (Lee and DeVore 1968:4; Lee 1968).

Within the limitations just set forth—that women's roles are never dominant over men's roles in any society—there is, nonetheless, great variation from one society to another in the status of women as a group compared to men, from equal (albeit different) to enormously unequal. Theoretically one might place all societies on a continuum designating the status of women as compared to men from equal at one pole to grossly unequal at the other pole. On such an imaginary continuum, I would perhaps place the Yanomamö of South America as reported by Napoleon Chagnon (1968) and the Tiwi of North Australia as reported by Hart and Pilling (1960) near the low-status pole. The Isthmus Zapotecs, I believe, would be near the high-status or equal pole. Where our own society would fall I am not prepared to state at the present time, although it would certainly be lower than Isthmus Zapotec.

On what basis a society determines the status of the sexes is far from clearly understood. We can no longer claim that men's higher status rests on their greater contributions to the subsistence base nor can we state that women's status tends toward the lower end of the hypothetical continuum in primitive hunting and gathering societies and toward the opposite pole in modern industrialized societies, although that has long been a popular ethnocentric assumption. Perhaps status according to sex has much to do with how much importance the society places on sex as a status marker compared to other status markers such as age or social class. Perhaps there is some relationship between status by sex and the value the society attaches to nonformalized roles in the public domain. Probably we shall eventually discover that a combination of many things are involved.

Nonformalized Roles

For the Isthmus Zapotecs, nonformalized roles play a very important part in the social system. But what is meant by nonformalized roles? Eric Wolf speaks of core and periphery structures in complex societies, three of which he designates as kinship, friendship, and patron-client relations. Although he focuses on structure rather than role and does not relate core and peripheral structures to the assignment of role by sex, he seems to have in mind something very similar to what I have called formalized and nonformalized roles. Wolf states (1966:2), "We thus note that the formal framework of economic and political power exists alongside or intermingled with various other kinds of informal structure which are interstitial, supplementary, parallel to it." Others have more explicitly referred to roles and to role assignment by sex. Riegelhaupt (1967), for example, distinguishes between formal and informal roles in a Portuguese village. Ernestine Friedl (1967) makes a similar distinction for Greek peasant society, and Aswad (1967) refers to key and peripheral roles of noblewomen in the Middle East.[3] It is probably not accidental that anthropologists concerned with role types as they relate to women's roles have often been those with research experience in peasant societies. This fact might suggest that nonformalized roles and informal structures are more important adaptive devices for peasants than for some other social types. But perhaps it is premature even to suggest such relationships when we know so little about nonformalized roles and informal structures in the various social systems.

Even in simpler social systems one frequently encounters in the ethnographies some reference to what appears to be women's nonformalized roles. The following description of the Tiwi of Northern Australia illustrates women's nonformalized roles in the political domain of a society of hunters-gatherers ruled by a male gerontocracy (Hart and Pilling 1960:52–53):

> The "game" was one of trying to win friends and increase prestige and influence over others. . . . The most concrete symbol of Tiwi success was the possession of surplus food, for this not only permitted its possessor to make gifts to others and throw large parties for which he picked up the check, but also gave him lots of leisure time to devote to social and political life. Since a man

[3] I owe much to several individuals who have contributed to the formulation of my role model. Riegelhaupt (1967) describes the formal and informal roles among Portuguese peasant women, and these seem to be rather close to my formalized-nonformalized role dichotomy. From Friedl (1967) I have borrowed the terms public and private domain but employ them in a somewhat different manner.

required a large number of women in his work force if he was to build up a surplus of food, in the final analysis it was control of women that was the most tangible index of power and influence. Women were the main currency of the influence struggle, the main "trumps" in the endless bridge game.

. . . To a smart Tiwi politician, wives or daughters were assets but so was his mother—if submissive to her son's wishes. So were his sisters—if amenable. A bachelor at the age of thirty who had several sisters was a lucky young man, especially if those sisters already had daughters to their current husbands. As successful old men used their infant daughters to gain influence and buy satellites, so young men used their mothers and their sisters—if they could. . . . The devious details of Tiwi prestige and influence operations are much easier to follow if one keeps in mind the crucial fact that the Tiwi men valued women as political capital available for investment in gaining the goodwill of other men more than they were interested in them as sexual partners. . . .

Women were, however, a form of capital that possessed the power of talking back to the investors. As daughters or as wives they were quite thoroughly subordinate to the wishes of their fathers or husbands, and Tiwi wives were as frequently and as brutally beaten by their husbands as wives in any other savage society. But as mothers and as sisters the women were not coerced by their sons and their brothers. On the contrary, sons or brothers wishing to use their mothers or their sisters in their political schemes . . . could only do so with the active collaboration of the women concerned. Tough-minded young widows could drive a hard bargain with their brothers as to where they remarried, since each needed the other to make the remarriage acceptable to the tribe at large and to beat down the other competitors (the dead husband's brothers, for example) who wished to control the remarriage of the widows. Young girls had no bargaining power but young widows had a good deal. Old mothers with influential senior sons were extremely powerful. Any affront to an old woman was an affront to her sons, and some of the strongest influence networks were alliances of several senior brothers, in which their old mother seemed to be the mastermind and the senior sons largely the enforcers of what the old mother and her middle-aged daughters (their sisters) had decided among themselves.

. . . Not as independent operators, but as behind-the-scenes allies of their sons and brothers, Tiwi mothers and sisters enjoyed much more essential freedom in their own careers as often-remarried widows than would appear at first sight in a culture which ostensibly treated all women as currency in the political careers of the men. No matter how males, both old and young, might connive, they were constantly aware that no remarriage of a widow could ever be arranged and made to stick unless the widow herself was agreeable.

In the above example, Tiwi women have a formalized role as "currency" in the political games of influence and prestige men play, clearly an inferior, powerless role. *But* mothers and sisters fill powerful nonformalized roles in the same game. This nonformalized political role of certain kin categories of women is not sufficiently pervasive to place Tiwi society very high on our hypothetical status continuum according to Hart and Pilling's account.[4] Women's nonformalized role is viewed by the men in fact as a hindrance rather than an aid to their political maneuvers. Perhaps there is some relationship between women's status and whether their nonformalized roles are viewed as complementing or competing with

[4] Goodale's account of women's roles in *Tiwi Wives* (1970) did not come to my attention until after the final draft of the case study was complete. On the basis of her data I would place the Tiwi somewhat above the Yanomamö (Chagnon) on the status of women continuum discussed in the text.

the formalized roles, although I have no crosscultural data to support such a suggestion.

Another example of women's nonformalized roles comes from an incident which occurred in a peasant community in Puebla, Mexico, as related by Elmendorf (1971):

> Facilities had been arranged for short-term loans which would allow the purchase of hybrid seed and fertilizer, which could easily be repaid from the promised doubled yield of the first crop. The farmers were enthusiastic at the presentation, but none followed through with a request for a loan. Dr. _____ explained that he finally learned from his field workers that the wives were not permitting their husbands to go into debt, and that as soon as the program was presented and explained to the women, loans were taken out.

In the Puebla community, women clearly have an important nonformalized role in economic decision making in the private domain. A number of examples could be cited from other sources. Friendship, for instance, could be considered a nonformalized role (or in Wolf's terms, part of the informal, interstitial structure) which occurs in most social systems. Friendship may be formalized to a certain degree in some social systems and nonformalized in others. Among the Isthmus Zapotecs, some friendship alliances may eventually evolve into the highly formalized role of compadre in which case the relationship changes from one of friendship to one of fictive kinship and the role changes from nonformalized to formalized.

FORMALIZED ROLES AND ISTHMUS ZAPOTEC WOMEN

An examination of the formalized roles in the Isthmus Zapotec public domain makes it clear that men and male formalized roles carry higher status than women and female formalized roles. The women of San Juan Evangelista confirm this daily by a hundred different acts and statements. It never occurs to them to resent this order of things. That is simply the way the universe was created. To question woman's status compared to that of man would be as absurd as to question why one must breathe to live. No woman of San Juan Evangelista has ever held nor ever expects to hold an office in the ayuntamiento of the municipio. My suggestion of the possibility always elicited at least a smile. More often women thought the idea hilarious. There were no women among the sixteen or more *xuanas* in the ex-distrito of El Centro (which includes San Juan Evangelista) in 1966–1967. No informants ever remembered any woman holding the office in the past, although the suggestion appeared to seem less absurd than a woman in the ayuntamiento probably because today the office of xuana is more figurative and ceremonial than political. Nor had any woman informants ever voted in a local election, but a number of men had not either.

Other evidence for the lower status of women in the public formalized domain includes the fact that the only women given the designation of comerciante in San Juan Evangelista are those who are half of a husband-wife merchant team. Comerciante, in fact, is the high-prestige formalized male role of which market place vendor is the low-prestige formalized female role, both in the public domain. These are not complementary roles nor are they competitive in actuality, although they could be considered so potentially. Turning to the fiesta system, more importance is attached to men's formalized role of contributor-participant than the same role of women. As evidence, men's contributions are called *cuotas* (assessments) and are always recorded while women's contributions are designated as *limosna* (alms) and are most often not recorded (although they are remembered nonetheless). Women pay men's cuotas in their absence or even after their death. Men never do this for women's limosna. Finally, women bear the brunt of the observation of strict mourning taboos. When a death occurs in the family, men and boys may resume their work almost immediately, but even if the family is depend-ent on a woman's earnings in the market place, she cannot sell there until forty days have passed. The strength of this restriction is illustrated in the following example which I witnessed:

> Petrona's mother died after a long and costly terminal illness. Petrona had not lived in her mother's solar since her marriage fifteen years earlier. When her mother fell ill Petrona had taken over the mother's pottery puesto in the market place to help out. During the illness of more than two years Petrona contributed part of the earnings from the puesto to her mother's expenses. Petrona's older sister, an unmarried viajera, had borne much of the expense and had been forced to stay with her mother so often that she was finding great difficulty making ends meet. When the mother died, income was badly needed to pay off debts and meet current expenses. Two weeks after the mother's death Petrona asked me what I thought about her reopening the pottery puesto. I told her I thought people would understand the situation, knowing the long terminal illness of her mother and the need to meet expenses. Although apprehensive about what people would say, she finally decided to go to the market place if I would stay with her to give her moral support. We opened the puesto at 7 A.M. the next day. None of her market neighbors seemed concerned and her customers expressed no dismay, surprise, or disapproval of her behavior, at least not overtly. Everyone seemed friendly and helpful, but Petrona was so certain that her selling after only two weeks would cause a scandal that by 10 A.M. she had developed a severe headache. She closed the puesto before noon and did not reopen it until after the forty-day mixa guétu. Her sister, the viajera, did not leave the solar of her mother until the mixa guétu.

NONFORMALIZED ROLES AND ISTHMUS ZAPOTEC WOMEN

Isthmus Zapotec women clearly have few powerful formalized roles in the public domain while the female half of complementary role pairs in either the public or private domain is always subordinate to the male role. This being the case, it may seem puzzling that I place Isthmus Zapotec society high on the status of women continuum. A thorough examination of the nonformalized roles of women will add clarification, I believe, because it is in the nonformalized roles that Isthmus Zapotec women play such a vital part in the social system.

As mentioned previously, violence is an expected male behavior pattern, especially dangerous when the man is intoxicated. Anger is an emotion which is always thought to be perilously close to the surface in the male personality, an emotion which can suddenly flare into violent acts. Women too are capable of anger, but a woman's anger is seen as less apt to result in violence and less threatening to community solidarity, since it is most often confined to the private domain. At least three presumptions about male behavior figure in women's assessment of social situations and the appropriate response either through an individual act or a nonformalized role. First, it is presumed, as stated above, that men will always react aggressively and violently when conflict arises between men. Second, it is presumed that all men will make sexual overtures to any woman, given the opportunity. Third, women presume that a husband will sooner or later wish to establish sexual relationships with one or more other women, perhaps ultimately creating a second family, which will divert resources from the first family. All such presumptions reflect a certain degree of reality and all are shared to some degree by both sexes, but many Zapotec men follow few or none of the presumed patterns. Perhaps the two most important factors in Isthmus Zapotec culture guiding people's behavior are fear of loss of life, health, and property (as discussed in a previous chapter) and the common presumptions about the nature of men. These two factors may give rise to the necessity and the opportunity for women to function in many nonformalized roles in the public as well as in the private domain. In other words, in Isthmus Zapotec society nonformalized roles may be considered an adaptive mechanism, and women thus may have an adaptive advantage, conferred by the total social system, in filling most effectively such nonformalized roles as those described herein.

I do not imply that women fill all nonformalized roles. Men almost certainly fill a number of important nonformalized roles in Isthmus Zapotec society. The political factions which seem to be endemic in the region function largely through male nonformalized roles, for example, although women also play nonformalized roles at times in the same arena. Since I was a woman investigating women's roles, the obvious result is a better understanding on my part of women's nonformalized roles.

Overt and Covert Nonformalized Roles

One final role distinction may be made which is not included in the role model represented in Fig. 8-1. I refer to a distinction between overt and covert nonformalized roles. Although such a distinction could be made also for formalized roles, for present purposes it is necessary only as it applies to nonformalized female roles in Isthmus Zapotec society. In general, overt roles are those in which behavior of the individual is known to all persons affected by such behavior and the behavior is socially acceptable. Friendship usually involves an overt role. Covert roles are those in which the performer wishes to keep his behavior secret from some other person or persons directly affected by such behavior, for whatever reason. Covert roles need not be illicit, although they sometimes may be, either within the society itself or in terms of the larger society which exercises punitive power. Covert roles may be manipulative rather than illicit, and manipulative roles may be employed for either malevolent or benevolent purposes. The nonformalized roles of Isthmus Zapotec women are most often overt, or they are covert roles for benevolent manipulative purposes, at least on the basis of my present knowledge.

Women's Overt Nonformalized Roles

In San Juan Evangelista the primitive communication system (no telephones, United Parcel Service, or daily newspaper) makes the roles of women as messengers and reporters of great importance to the menfolk while the pervasive fears of envy and violence make the roles of women as intermediaries and agents no less essential.[5] In this connection it must be remembered that most men are away from the pueblo during daylight hours six or seven days a week, working in their fields or elsewhere. Furthermore, women's marketing activities allow the movement of women almost anywhere in the pueblo or in El Centro at almost any hour without arousing suspicion while such movements of men would be much more noticeable and therefore very possibly suspect. As they make their daily excursions to and from the market places and one another's solares on marketing business, women can carry messages mentally and articles not intended for the public eye buried in their headbaskets or handbaskets. Women usually function as messengers and reporters for the convenience of the menfolk of the household as in the following examples from my field notes:

Case 1   Alvaro has a pair of *toritos* ready to put out on a three-year contract. He has discussed the matter two or three times with Isabel (his wife) and Doña Teresa (his elderly mother). The problem is that he knows of several men who would probably want the toritos, including Jesús (Alvaro's brother-in-law), who doesn't know Alvaro has the toritos, it seems. Contracting them to Jesús is out because of his binges, during one of which he is reported to have left a team of oxen belonging to Doña Teresa without feed and water for several days. When discovered, they were almost dead, according to Doña T. Alvaro doesn't want to arouse Jesús' envy or add to some already apparent resentment on the part of Jesús. This morning it seems he has solved the problem. He told Isabel to stop by the solar of Apolinar on her way to the plaza to see if they might want the team. I suspect a factor in his decision is the location of Apolinar's *terrenos* near Santa Rita, far removed from the fields of Jesús which would facilitate transfer of the toritos without Jesús' knowledge.

Isabel carried the message to the solar of Apolinar. As it turned out, Apolinar did not need the toritos, but it was arranged that the son of one of his compadres should take them. The latter lived at El Jacal, again well removed from the resentful eyes of Jesús. By prearrangement, Apolinar's compadre and his son arrived by truck at the solar of Alvaro a few nights later, signed the contract, and then, accompanied by Alvaro, proceeded to el monte to pick up the calves.

Case 2   Late this afternoon while I was at Doña R.'s, Inez (her married daughter) arrived unexpectedly to warn Jose Luis not to be seen with his partner, Victor Manuel F. The rumor is circulating that someone is looking for one of Victor's brothers, who has suddenly disappeared. She doesn't know of the source of the trouble or any details yet.

The background data for the above incident is as follows: Jose Luis had just recently bought a small herd of cattle in partnership with Victor who was a distant

---

[5] Several public address systems, located in widely separated parts of the pueblo, charge a fee for each public announcement. Most public announcements concern weddings, fiestas, deaths, elopements, and lost and found animals.

relative. They were not particularly close friends. The partnership had evolved when Victor had encountered a "deal" on a herd in Chahuites (about 100 kilometers from San Juan Evangelista) and did not have enough cash to swing the deal alone. In casting about for a partner he approached Jose Luis who happened to have the cash on hand and had, in fact, been considering buying some cattle. When the rumor involving Victor's brother reached Inez' ears probably no one but the immediate families of the two partners knew that they were in partnership on the cattle. The reasons for Inez' warning and the urgency with which she brought the report to Jose Luis can be best understood by following the cattle partnership through to its dissolution two years later.

A short time after Inez' warning to her brother, another of Victor's brother (not the one reported to have disappeared) and a boy passenger in his truck were ambushed and killed on the streets of San Juan. Immediately after this unfortunate incident, Victor Manuel left the municipio. Jose Luis was stuck with the care and expense of the entire herd of cattle which he could not sell without his partner's signature. About a year later Jose Luis went north and found employment, turning the management of the cattle over to one of his sisters, whom he instructed to keep trying to get Victor's address from some of his relatives so that the needed signature could be obtained. Finally, two years after the beginning of the cattle partnership, Victor's mother, who had also left San Juan Evangelista, returned for a short visit during which time Jose Luis' sister and Victor Manuel's mother were able to dissolve the partnership by proxy. In this case, the role of women as agents in the cattle partnership was crucial to its successful and eventual dissolution.

Case 3   When Don Guillermo's aged mother died, I drove him out to the cemetery to arrange with the caretaker for a burial plot. To "do the talking" he chose a young woman relative whom I had not met previously, although there were several male relatives and compadres in his solar at the time. Don G. was incapacitated by profound grief from making his own arrangements since the trip to the cemetery was made within two hours of his mother's death. Don G. wanted his mother buried in one of two spaces next to the chapel, both of which were reserved, according to the caretaker. The agent, Catalina, did all the talking on Don Guillermo's behalf. After several minutes of bargaining with the caretaker, she pulled $50 out of the waistband of her skirt and handed it to the caretaker. He said it was not enough, but accepted reluctantly after Catalina reminded him that the burial space was, after all, only temporary. (When the family for whom the space was reserved needed it, Don Guillermo's mother's body would be moved, a common practice in San Juan.) Catalina also made arrangements for the grave diggers, and she and I brought to the cemetery and served the meal to which they were entitled when finished.

Several months later an occasion arose during which I could ask Don Guillermo why he had chosen Catalina, who was about thirty and a very attractive woman, to make arrangements at the cemetery. He replied that bargaining with a pretty woman makes it difficult to answer in the negative. But, as I later learned, Catalina's husband's family was well-to-do and Catalina herself had inherited a respectable sum of money, both of which contributed to her status. There were very probably ties of some sort (patron-client, landlord-renter, compadre, or other) between the cemetery caretaker and someone in Catalina's family or the family of her husband which made it even more difficult to say no to Catalina than her pretty face, but what such ties were or even if they existed I never learned.

Another overt nonformalized role which women fill concerns maintaining order at the fiestas. When asked the question of whose responsibility it is to maintain order at the fiestas, informants invariably reply that the mayordomo appoints two or three men who usually serve without pay, each taking a turn for an agreed upon period of time. This is correct, except that the information is incomplete. What has been elicited are the formalized public male roles. Observation indicates that the formal policing action takes place outside the fiesta itself. These men guard the entrances to the fiesta and maintain order among the crowds of men that inevitably gather in the streets surrounding the place of the fiesta where portable cantinas are set up to sell beer. The complementary nonformalized role of maintaining order within the fiesta where the guests are all invited friends, compadres, and kinsmen of the hosts is generally, perhaps always, filled by women. My data, based on attendance at perhaps twenty-five fiestas of various kinds, suggests that whenever a male guest, encouraged by too much mezcal, begins to behave improperly, an elderly kinswoman intervenes. Commonly the man will leave his seat on the men's bench and begin to dance among the women. This is considered improper behavior since only women dance at fiestas except in two or three rigidly prescribed ritual contexts when certain men dance.[6] The woman, perhaps his aunt, his grandmother, or on occasion his madrina (fictive kin), first tries gentle persuasion to get the man to return to his seat. If this fails, she resorts to somewhat stronger statements about honor and shame. If the man continues to resist her efforts, something I witnessed only once, the woman may maneuver him near an exit and forcibly push him out where the "official guards" take over.

Perhaps the most frequent context of women's overt nonformalized roles concerns sexual aggression. As has been pointed out in previous pages, the household's honor depends on the honor of its women. Any threat to the women's honor, therefore, demands action by the male household head against the transgressor. But the primary responsibility of avoiding and averting sexual overtures is placed on the women themselves. Women cooperate in overt nonformalized roles to protect one another from sexual aggression. Within the community what might be interpreted as improper advances on the part of a man are invariably associated with drinking. Therefore women avoid any possibility of interaction with a drunken man by signaling one another of the approach of a borracho on the public streets, by ducking into one another's doorways and tienditas, and by many other avoidance techniques. It seems to be an unwritten law among Isthmus Zapotec women that women stand united in the face of the threat of any kind of unwanted or improper attention from a man, whether the man is stranger or brother. Such cooperative roles go beyond kinswomen and even beyond friends and neighbors. Any group of Zapotec women, whether in the market place, in

---

[6] At fiestas certain important men dance the Zandunga. Both sexes dance at the same time and sometimes in pairs but without bodily contact. The Zandunga is a ritual dance performed at certain points during the fiestas.

the streets, or at a fiesta, whether known to one another or complete strangers, seems to close ranks spontaneously whenever there appears to be the slightest possibility of a threat to someone's "honor." When I was still a stranger in San Juan and did not know the rules of behavior, I several times found myself beckoned into the solar of a woman I had never seen before because a weaving, stumbling figure was approaching, perhaps still half a block away.[7] A male informant claimed that women also cooperate in arranging and concealing one another's trysts with lovers. I have no doubt that this kind of cooperation occurs, but it seems either to have been rare or absent among the women I knew best, none of whom mentioned it.

Nonformalized cooperative roles among women are not limited to protection from men, however. Women cooperate in watching one another's puestos in the market place, in helping a neighbor carry her bultos to the bus, in reporting undesirable actions of one another's teen-age daughters, in reciprocal child care, and in other ways. Such cooperation may but does not necessarily run along kin lines. In one instance, the male household heads of adjoining solares had not been on speaking terms for several years, yet the wives continued reciprocal economic transactions.

Women's Covert Nonformalized Roles

Sometimes it is difficult or impossible to draw a fine line of distinction between women's covert and overt nonformalized roles in Isthmus Zapotec culture. In Case 4 which follows, for example, what began as covert behavior on the part of the women actually became overt in regard to Abel when he learned of the incident before it was concluded. Abel acknowledged the women's roles and gave his tacit approval by leaving the solar when he inadvertently learned of the trouble. He remained away until plenty of time had elapsed for the women to complete their plans. Usually covert roles of Zapotec women, or at least those known to me, have the tacit approval of the menfolk they seek to manipulate. If not, they are viewed as being in the man's best interests and would have either his approval or approval of his peers if known.

Case 4   Abel, a bachelor in his mid-thirties, lived in the solar where he was born with his elderly widowed mother, Doña Maria. The house was recognized by the entire family, including married siblings living elsewhere, as belonging to Abel. He had built it bit by bit over the years with his earnings as a bank teller, fulfilling a prophecy made by his father at Abel's birth. Abel was the fourth of five living siblings, and only surviving son of Doña Maria. All the sisters were married and living in other solares. Doña Maria's health had begun to fail, and since she had no daughter-in-law to care for her, one of Abel's

---

[7] During one phase of fieldwork I traveled with Jonsa and Elena, cousins who regularly sold Isthmus products in a market place some 350 miles distant. We spent from ten days to two weeks in the distant market place on each occasion. On one occasion they concealed me for two days from an overly persistent suitor by stationing a ten-year-old sentry at the market entrance. Whenever the man approached, the signal was passed and I beat a hasty retreat out the rear entrance or hid in another woman's puesto. On another occasion Jonsa and Elena hid me from further verbal assaults by a male market vendor after the latter became abusive in language over U.S. involvement in Vietnam. In this case, the signal was passed whenever he left his puesto, headed our way, at which time I would duck into the neighboring woman's puesto where I could be neatly hidden from view by her pottery.

married sisters frequently came to clean up the solar and wait on Doña Maria, sometimes staying several days.

Abel had been planning for some time to install windows in the two back rooms of the house to improve air circulation in the solar. Doña Maria opposed his plan. Windows with glass panes are rare in San Juan Evangelista mainly because of the open invitation they present to rock throwers and little boys with slingshots. In this case, however, the windows would open onto a big corral back of the house where Abel kept his oxen and horse. The footpath behind the corral was 60 yards or more from the house and the corral itself was enclosed with a rail fence. Abel reasoned correctly that it would be almost impossible for anyone to hurl a missile through the windows while passing on the footpath. He proceeded with his plan.

About two weeks after the windows were installed, Abel's brother-in-law arrived unannounced at the solar in a grossly inebriated state while Abel's sister Angela, wife of the inebriated man, was serving dinner to her ailing mother. An argument ensued which ended by Abel throwing his brother-in-law, Justino, into the street and telling him never to set foot inside the solar again. Abel, pale with rage, left the solar a short time later and did not return until dawn. Angela spent the night with her mother in the solar. Sometime during the night Justino climbed into the corral at the rear of the house and heaved rocks through most of the forty or so panes in the two new windows. Fortunately, the women were able to keep Abel from learning of the incident when he returned home briefly before going to work the following morning. When I talked to them later the same morning, they were terrified at the prospect of Abel finding out before the damage had been repaired. Both Doña Maria and Angela feared that a tragedy was imminent, one apt to prove fatal to one or both men. In order to do everything they could to avert tragedy, the women went into action as soon as Abel left for his job.

Word was sent via a neighbor girl (who was also kin to the family) to Abel's two sisters who resided in the pueblo. Both of them arrived at their mother's solar shortly thereafter. The plan was to keep Abel and Justino apart at all costs. Margarita, the eldest sister, acting on behalf of her ailing mother, filed a formal complaint with the presidente which resulted in Justino's arrest and incarceration. With Justino safely behind bars and thus protected for the time being from Abel's justifiable rage an almost audible collective sigh of relief settled over Doña Maria's solar.

The next step was to have the windows repaired as quickly as possible. The women felt it was imperative that the windows be completely repaired by nightfall when Abel returned from his job. Doña Maria thought Abel's rage (that is, the threat to his honor and to his position as household head) would be less if no visual reminders of the episode remained when it finally came to his attention. A condition of Justino's release from jail was that he pay for the damages in full, a rather dim possibility considering his financial insolvency. Nevertheless, Doña Maria sent for a repairman to come and give an estimate of the cost of repairs. Abel's second married sister, Jovita, then went to the solar of one of Justino's several sisters with the information. About two hours later Justino's youngest sister, an unmarried girl in her early twenties, arrived at Doña Maria's solar with $150 which she gave to Doña M., promising to return later with the remaining needed sum, $50.

Abel returned home unexpectedly at noon and thus learned of the whole affair (probably he had already heard of it before he returned). Outwardly he remained calm and without uttering a word he turned on his heel and left the solar. He remained away for two days. By that time the windows were repaired, Justino was out of jail, and to my knowledge, the affair was never mentioned again by anyone concerned.

Justino's bold attack on Abel's property after the initial altercation was an open challenge to Abel's honor, to his position as head of the household, and to his formalized role of protector of his mother and sisters. It demanded retribution. Abel, although enraged, obviously wished to avoid bloodshed if possible. The cooperation of the women kinfolk of each of the two men made it possible for both to save face while avoiding the volatile face-to-face encounter the mores of the culture demanded.[8] It might be argued that the women of Abel's household acted on his behalf because he had no male kin to act for him, but the argument would not be valid in the case of Justino whose father and brother both lived in San Juan Evangelista. Although Justino and his brother maintained close personal ties, often cooperatively working their fields and exchanging labor and tools, it was not the brother but the three sisters who raised and delivered the $200 to Doña Maria.

Cases 5 and 6 both occurred prior to my fieldwork and were recounted to me in casual conversations. Possibly having interesting implications about the importance of nonformalized covert roles to the women themselves is the fact that Case 5 was actually told to me at least three different times by different women in the kin group. The incident, not particularly dramatic, had occurred more than two years earlier.

Case 5 When Abel's youngest sister married, it was his duty as head of the household to fill the role of bride's father who was deceased. Being the only brother of four sisters, Abel had always taken his role as protector of his sisters very seriously, particularly the youngest sister, Felipa, who was eight years his junior. Doña Maria, the mother, apparently perceived that Abel might have difficulty making the sudden role switch, especially since the wedding was the aftermath of Felipa's elopement which could have been interpreted as an assault to Abel's honor or as a failure on his part to control the improper behavior of his sister. Abel was a rather serious young man who ordinarily did not drink or frequent cantinas. None of the family had ever seen him inebriated. The small wedding fiesta demanded that Abel drink a rather large quantity of mezcal in the form of ritual toasts within a few hours. Doña Maria feared he might become hostile and even violent under such conditions. To avoid potential trouble, a plan was devised. During the fiesta the womenfolk would keep Abel under close surveillance. At the first sign of threatening behavior on Abel's part, Doña Maria, physically too fragile to become involved herself, was to give the signal to Margarita, the eldest sister several years Abel's senior, and to Faustina, a remote cousin of Margarita's age who possessed the added advantage of sturdy build. Margarita and Faustina were to flank Abel inconspicuously, laughing and joking, and sort of playfully dance him into a small adjoining bedroom, get him into the hammock, leave, and lock the door. The plan was carried out successfully. Abel never learned of it and still wonders, according to the women, how he came to be in the room where he awoke the next morning.

The last example of women's covert nonformalized roles is interesting because it was recounted by an elderly woman informant in the course of reconstructing her life history spontaneously at my request. The incident had occurred more than 30 years prior to my fieldwork, and it is possible that the informant, Doña Isabel,

---

[8] Actually this is a general Latin American cultural attitude and not peculiar to Isthmus Zapotec culture.

did not remember details precisely as they occurred. The informant obviously recalled Case 6 as a traumatic crisis in the course of her early married life.

Case 6   Around 1932 Doña Isabel was a young mother of two little daughters, living in the rear section of her mother-in-law's solar. Her husband by common-law marriage seems to have been ten or twelve years her senior. I estimate Doña Isabel was about twenty-five years old at the time. Her eldest child was perhaps two years old, the other a *criatura*. One day her husband came home and announced he had found another woman, a *cantinera* in San Jacinto, with whom he was going to live. This placed Doña Isabel in a vulnerable position economically because her own father had strongly opposed her decision to live with her husband without benefit of a wedding ceremony. Now she could not turn to him or her brothers for help as would normally have been the case. She had no resources of her own and two infants to care for and support. Had she married in the Church she would have been able to count on her kinsmen and the couple's padrinos to bring pressure to bear on her errant husband to comply with his obligations. Doña Isabel did not accept her husband's decision passively, although he apparently began living with the cantinera and was absent from his mother's solar for days on end. She had a strong ally in her mother-in-law, however, who was incensed by her son's behavior. Whenever Celso, the husband, did come home, his mother would hide Doña Isabel and the children in the rear of her own house and tell her son they had moved out permanently and she did not know where they were. The two women carried on the ruse successfully for some time. Finally, Doña Isabel met him at the door on one of his visits, announced she had just returned, and stated she was willing to stay but only if he discontinued his relationship with the cantinera. Doña Isabel recounts that he agreed because he did not want to lose his children.

Isabel and Celso remained together for the rest of Celso's life, and produced seven more children. When I asked if the reconciliation marked the end of her marital troubles, she replied, "Oh, no. We had disagreements many times but Celso's mother always took my part as long as she lived."

SUMMARY

In this chapter, I have tried to demonstrate through case material how women's nonformalized roles function to maintain the integrity of the household, to avoid conflict and violence, and more generally to add oil to the social machinery in a system where there exists a high level of fear and anxiety.

Both sexes recognize the importance of women's behavior in these nonformalized roles. At the same time the people themselves are sometimes unaware of the patterning and frequency of such behavior which marks it as role behavior rather than random idiosyncratic situational behavior. The importance of women's nonformalized roles to the viability of the social system can scarcely be overemphasized. A man without womenfolk to "run interference" through the hazardous maze of social relations would be at a great disadvantage compared to the man with several kinswomen, those married into other households as well as those in his own solar. One wonders if Jose Luis of Case 2 would have been the innocent victim of an assassin's bullet had he not been warned of impending trouble by his married sister. While women's nonformalized roles operate mainly through kinship (one of the informal structures recognized by Wolf), in the Isthmus Zapotec system it is the fact of sex rather than kinship which makes such roles possible, the fact that women operate in a social universe separate from men and therefore are privy to information which men either do not or may not circulate among themselves, and the fact that certain types of movement and courses of action are open only to women.

9 / Conclusion

IMAGES, PUBLIC AND PRIVATE

There is a popular stereotype in Mexican national culture of Isthmus Zapotec women as assertive, dominant individuals who favor strong language and ribald behavior, supposedly in contrast to other Mexican peasant women. The grain of truth on which the stereotype is founded is probably based on the women's reaction to strangers, especially those of the opposite sex and of the dominant mestizo culture. Conditions of life of Isthmus Zapotec women make it necessary for them to move about in public places while a general Latin American cultural ideal is that a "lady" rarely if ever appears in public places. In a social system in which family honor hinges on women's virtue and in which women must be free to pursue their buying-selling ventures in many public places, while upholding the family's honor at the same time, it becomes imperative that women behave in ways designed to leave no doubt in anyone's mind as to their virtue. Thus Isthmus Zapotec girls are socialized to rebuff improper and undesirable attention. Members of both sexes greatly admire "a woman who defends herself" by devastatingly insulting remarks directed toward would-be lotharios. Whenever I complained to informants of unpleasantly familiar encounters with men in El Centro, in Oaxaca, or elsewhere, I was told that it was my own fault because I did not defend myself.[1]

In the more intimate contexts of neighborhood and solar, women's behavior is quite different from their stereotyped public image. On the intragroup level of social relations, I found women modest, decorous, considerate of others, gentle, empathetic, and indulgent of children and oldsters. These same characteristics also mark the behavior of Zapotec men under normal conditions and in similar contexts. Thus, the important dichotomy between intragroup and intergroup behavior must be clearly distinguished in any discussion of the behavior of the people of San Juan Evangelista. Whereas in intragroup relationships there are strong sanctions against conflict and violence, such sanctions are relaxed when intergroup relationships are involved, especially when actions of the outgroup

[1] I did eventually learn the technique of "defending" myself and found it most effective. However, I always felt it was a little unjust in my case because my atypical behavior according to phenotype could not be anticipated.

are perceived as threats to members of the community. In San Juan Evangelista adults of either sex will come to the aid of any member of the community who seems to be threatened by outsiders. Women are often actively involved in repelling threats to the homefront simply because they are more apt to be present in the pueblo when such threats occur than are the menfolk. It is probably also true that women can act aggressively toward the dominant mestizo power structure with less fear of reprisals than can men. I was told that mestizo police from El Centro sometimes pursue and try to intimidate San Juan Evangelista boys and that when this occurs the women of the pueblo rush to the boys' defense, threatening the policemen with *palos* and using abusive language. Although I did not witness any such incidents during my stay, corroborative evidence abounds.[2]

It may seem paradoxical that in a culture where roles are clearly delineated by sex, the people are not overly concerned with deviations from such roles nor with sex as a status marker. In San Juan Evangelista, one is first a human being, an individual, and only second and incidentally a man or a woman. While the sexes are usually segregated, perform different tasks, wear distinct clothing, and behave differently, none of these differences is viewed as marking the essential inferiority of one sex in relation to the other. Women do not do agricultural work except to help with or direct the picking of fruit on occasion, yet most of them know enough about agriculture to manage their land with hired labor should it become necessary. Men usually do not do women's work, but this seems to be more because there are women and girls to do it than because of any strict aversion to "doing women's work." One father did the laundry by hand for a large family for a period of time when the mother was ill and no hired help was available. Nobody thought his actions unusual, and it was obvious that doing the laundry posed no threat to his virility. A man much admired seems to have been an individual with transsexual attributes who resided in the solar of a widower with a large family of small children and "acted just like a mother to those children" for a number of years until he died some time prior to my fieldwork. This man seems to have actually taken over the role of wife and mother in the family, even to making tortillas, a skill which requires years of training and is almost never taught to boys.

The phenomenon of *machismo*, so often cited as a male characteristic in Latin American cultures, seems to be largely absent in intra-group relations in Zapotec culture. Where such behavior is evident, it is negatively sanctioned. A man who acts *muy macho* is derided as an overbearing bully, and a woman who mistreats or takes advantage of one weaker than she, is similarly criticized (for example, a mother who strikes her child).

Comparing Isthmus Zapotec women to women in my own middle-class United States culture, I discovered some surprising differences. I have already noted the esprit de corps among Zapotec women, something distressingly lacking among ourselves. This attitude, which goes beyond kinship and beyond ethnicity, allows

---

[2] A recent incident involved a dispute between the men of San Juan Evangelista and some mestizo lessees of the municipio's land for commercial farming in which the lessees and some officials from El Centro were held hostages for several hours in San Juan Evangelista. Although they managed to escape eventually, they were met at the exit to the pueblo by a hostile group of residents, men and women, armed with clubs and rocks.

women to cooperate in many situations where it would be impossible for men to do so. But apart from this, Zapotec women seem to possess a self-identity as part of a universal sisterhood. They assume, naively to be sure, that their goals, aspirations, and desires are shared by all womankind. They do not view themselves as competing with other women for men's favors, they do not seek their own self-identity through men, nor do they view themselves as dependent upon men to any greater extent than men are dependent upon women. In San Juan Evangelista survival requires the efforts of every able person in the household. No member's contribution is belittled or considered insignificant.

Perhaps because they are secure in their position as women, Isthmus Zapotec women rarely express jealousy toward other women over men. Whereas, on the basis of experience in my own culture, I expected that my presence would arouse sexual jealousy and resentment in wives and sweethearts, I found no evidence that this ever occurred even in the few instances in which I spent a great deal of time talking to a husband alone.[3] Conversely, my interaction with the mestizo population of El Centro was marked by obvious distrust and jealousy on the part of wives, notwithstanding the fact that my interaction with mestizo men was both limited and public. I believe this difference in behavior between Zapotec and mestizo women marks a fundamental difference in status of women and women's self-image in the two groups.

Zapotec women do express jealousy of women's friendships with other women, often in a lighthearted, half-joking manner. I have no explanation for this other than that friendship is a highly valued and avidly sought relationship for the entire culture, but one which appears to be difficult to maintain outside the kin group. Perhaps that is a compelling reason for the great viability of compadrazgo which cements friendship relations into more binding and formal fictive kin ties. I found no evidence of latent or overt homosexuality in women's expressions of jealousy.

Another admirable quality of Isthmus Zapotec women is their ability to refrain from open criticism and disdain toward other women, in fact toward anyone. I spent untold hours listening to and taking part in casual conversations among women, sometimes large groups gathered to prepare food for a fiesta, sometimes groups of market vendors and their customers, more often small groups of kinswomen or neighbors, and frequent and extended conversations stretching over months with two unrelated families whose members acted as key informants. The occasions on which women expressed criticism, disdain, or derision toward another person were so rare that they still stand out in my memory.[4] Aside from one family who was ostracized for nonparticipation in the community and seemed to be fair game for disdainful remarks, there were two cases of suspected witchcraft brought

[3] At first I carefully avoided such situations since I did not want to alienate the women, but later I found that the women did not object in those few cases where a husband had the time and desire to talk with me at length.

[4] I recorded negative remarks about others as a matter of course, anticipating that such remarks contained important clues about factions, points of disagreement, and conflict within the community. While there is certainly much factionalism, disagreement, and conflict, I did not find women's gossip very helpful in learning of them.

to my attention when the supposed victims confided their *desconfianza* in the "witch." One informant denounced a distant kinsman in private conversation, a person whom she considered to be overly concerned with status and self-aggrandizement. Another informant once expressed to me privately her envy of another woman's pregnancy, a remark which would have been interpreted as dangerous and threatening to the pregnant woman had it been overheard by anyone.

On the other hand, women seemed often to harbor deep wounds from what they considered to be slights and favoritism to other kin displayed by primary female relatives, especially mothers and sisters, and there was evidence of resentment and rivalry between some opposite-sex adolescent siblings. It may be that unfavorable comments directed toward persons outside the immediate kin groups are rare because they can be interpreted as threats, as expressions of envy, as ill wishes which can cause actual harm.

CHANGES

Peasant societies are usually considered culturally conservative and slow to change. By modern standards changes have come slowly to Zapotec campesinos, yet Zapotecs have always been a changing people, and they have demonstrated through centuries their great ability to adapt to changing conditions. Despite their fierce independence, Isthmus Zapotecs have not been politically autonomous for five, perhaps six or more, centuries. Nonetheless they have managed to survive as an ethnically distinct population. They readily adopted a vast number of sixteenth-century Spanish culture traits, and they adapted their own culture to the demands of colonial rule. Changes wrought by Mexican Independence and the more recent Revolution have been extensive. If colonial-era technology and behavior patterns linger on, it is not because Isthmus Zapotecs reject other patterns out of hand but rather that their present system remains viable in their present environment.

It has been claimed by some that women are the most conservative segment of peasant communities, although there is considerable evidence to the contrary. Certainly the women of San Juan Evangelista have accepted new ideas and adopted new ways as eagerly as have the men, perhaps with even more enthusiasm. Several decades ago women saw the great advantages in treadle sewing machines and mechanical nixtamal mills. Today they buy blenders when economic circumstances permit because they have recognized the blender as one of the very few small appliances which has great utility in Zapotec kitchens. Sometimes women have adopted new gadgets only to discard them later as unsuitable. The kerosene stove is an example. Very few are used in San Juan Evangelista today but nonfunctioning stoves are often to be seen abandoned in a corner of the solar. Their single advantage over the conventional stone hearth seems to be a quick fire. Women found them expensive to operate and the odor offensive. Impure fuel and improper care and cleaning induced excessive smoking and malfunction, and people complained that food cooked on kerosene stoves tasted like kerosene. Women's costume, although changing in style, has remained basically traditional because of its utility, cultural ideals of modesty, and attractiveness.

Today alternatives become increasingly apparent, increasingly possible. Matrons in San Juan Evangelista ask my opinion about cutting their hair and adopting modern dress. A young woman going to Mexico City to visit relatives decides to buy two or three *vestidos* to wear there so people will not stare at her. Another young woman *viajera* considers learning to drive and buying a Volkswagen to make her selling trips to distant markets. The daughters of a prosperous *carnicera* have no interest in learning their mother's trade because by mestizo standards it is "low class." They prefer to prepare themselves for low-paying white-collar jobs, although the majority of such jobs are presently filled by young men.

Public education stresses national mestizo culture and ideology. Thus far, the effects on Isthmus Zapotec culture have been minimal because the education level has been low (relatively few children attending school relatively few years). As the education level increases and more children are formally educated, the adoption of mestizo values is likely to be massive, for already Zapotec campesinos accept the judgment that middle-class mestizo culture is superior to their own. A few educated Zapotecs urge the people to conserve las costumbres—the language, traditional dress, music, poetry, rituals, storytelling, and oratory skills. I too hope that such traditions can be preserved, but even more importantly I would hope the people can preserve those essential values and attitudes which give to Isthmus Zapotec culture its nobility. Among such values and attitudes, I would include a belief in the essential humanity of every individual, an insistence on the right of every person to maintain his dignity as a human being regardless of ethnic or class differences, respect for the aged, a profound empathy with and concern for ill and dying or otherwise unfortunate people, an attitude of equality between the sexes, tenderness and indulgence toward children which somehow avoids the pitfalls of excessive permissiveness, and an indomitable independence of spirit.

ISTHMUS ZAPOTECS IN AN ENLARGING WORLD

It is often said that with modern transportation and modern communication the world is becoming smaller. In microcosm the same things that minimize the world enlarge formerly isolated people's world view. For the Isthmus Zapotecs, their world is widening through more cultural contacts with the modern, industrialized world. It is difficult to imagine the tremendous influence the United States exerts on the Isthmus Zapotecs and other Third World peoples. Although almost no Isthmus Zapotecs contracted to work in the United States during the years of the *bracero* program, even illiterate campesinos have great admiration for the United States because of the spread of U.S. technology—automobiles, farm equipment, all types of machinery and appliances, wrinkle-free clothing, and many other "modern miracles."[5] None of these things does the ordinary Zapotec campesino hope to possess, but he admires them nonetheless through exposure by films,

---

[5] I do not know why so few Isthmus men contracted into the bracero program. It is in strong contrast to the situation among other Zapotec communities in the Valley and Sierra of Oaxaca, where more than half the adult men in some communities are reported to have been braceros.

tourists, and U.S. construction firms which have worked in the area. The space program and moon voyages, of course, have escaped no one's attention. On my last visit to the Isthmus women asked me if it was true as rumored that the space flights had caused the disastrous hurricanes and floods from which the region was just recovering.

The people admire the United States and they also fear us. Perhaps, they reason, the United States still covets the Isthmus of Tehuantepec as the site of an interocean canal. Who knows when our armies might move in and take over their homeland? On their radios, Isthmus Zapotecs receive an English-language station which broadcasts from Guatemala. Many people have traveled through Guatemala on pilgrimages. They have seen the English-language billboards, U.S.-built highways, gasoline stations of U.S. companies, and U.S. products everywhere. Most uneducated people believe that Guatemala is a possession of the United States.

The people assume that gringos are perfect, that the United States is utopia. Often they said, "But you don't have any poor people in the United States," and when I tried to explain otherwise, they simply could not believe it. Yes, if my friends from San Juan Evangelista were to visit the United States, they would be shocked and disillusioned by many things. They would never be able to comprehend our neglect, disregard, and segregation of the elderly nor would they be able to understand that in a developed economy of materialistic affluence, poverty may include such "luxuries" as automobiles and television sets and yet comprise a more dehumanizing and humiliating experience than the poverty they know. Nor could my Isthmus Zapotec friends comprehend our preoccupation with youth and youthfulness or the isolation of close kin in illness and death. But perhaps the most unnerving of all would be our "new morals."

Now the people's life conditions are changing more rapidly than perhaps ever before. The subsistence base is expanding perceptibly and survival is becoming a little less difficult year by year.[6] As new alternatives appear and old behavior patterns become less satisfactory, less attractive, and more difficult to follow, Isthmus Zapotec culture will change. In the process, one wonders if those positive values of individual worth and dignity, of complementary but equally valued sex roles, of compassion and empathy which all the world might profitably emulate, will be able to survive.

---

[6] In a sample survey I asked about fifty household heads if in their opinion their economic position had improved in the past decade. All answers were affirmative and usually definitely so.

Glossary

Agua potable: Water purified for household use.
Ahijado: Godchild.
Aire: "Bad" air associated with night and able to cause illness. Elsewhere often called *mal aire*.
Ambulante: Roving, nonpermanent market vendor with no regular space in the market place.
Anisado: Anise-flavored brandy.
Atole: Maize-flour gruel.
Ayuntamiento: Municipal government.
Baile: Dance.
Barrio: Quarter, neighborhood, subsection of pueblo.
Baul: Wooden trunk, usually with four legs and handsomely carved.
Borracho: Drunken; a drunken man.
Buena gente: Fine people.
Bulto: Package, baggage, cargo.
Butaca: Low wood chair with slat seat and high back forming a continuous curve.
Cacao: Cocoa.
Calor: Invisible property of recently deceased persons which can cause illness and death by contagion.
Campesino: Peasant.
Cantina: Tavern, saloon.
Cantinera: Woman owner or operator of a cantina.
Cargador: Porter.
Carnicera: Vendor of fresh meat, one of the few types of selling considered to be a specialization.
Carreta: Oxcart.
Cargo: Office; voluntary religious office.
Cebu: Humped breed of cattle introduced from Asia.
Celoso: Jealous.
Cesto: Large basketry container, usually about the shape and size of a small oil drum.
Chile ancho: A variety of chile pepper.
Choza: Small dwelling of reeds and thatch.
Cohete: Firecracker, rocket.
Comadre: Ritual co-mother.
Comerciante: Merchant or businessman, usually having a number of different sources of income.
Compadre: Ritual co-father.
Confianza: Confidence, trust.
Copal: Incense derived from tree resin.
Coraje: Anger; illness caused by emotion of anger.
Cordoncillo: An herb often used for curative purposes.
Corredor: Veranda, roofed passageway across front of house.
Corresponder: To respond, reciprocate.
Costumbres (las):   "The customs," a frequent phrase referring to Zapotec customs, especially those of ceremonial nature.
Criatura: Young infant.
Criollo: Local breed of plant or animal.

Cuota: Men's ritual monetary contribution, commonly $5.

Curandera: Woman curer.

Desconfianza: Distrust.

Ejido: Communal land ownership established after the Mexican Revolution.

Espanto: Fright.

Ex-distrito: Territorial subdivision of state, encompassing but having only partial political jurisdiction over several municipios.

Fletero: Truck driver, motor-freight hauler.

Gringa: A woman from the United States, any foreign woman of European phenotype.

Gueezé: Pinol, maize-flour gruel; the dry sweetened maize flour alone.

Hectarea: An area of land measuring 2.47 acres.

Huipil: Woman's unfitted blouse.

Huipil grande: White-pleated lace head covering worn for certain ritual occasions.

Invitados (los):   Invited guests at fiesta.

Istmeño: A native inhabitant of the Isthmus of Tehuantepec.

Ixtle: Plant fiber, used for cordage, mats, hammocks, and other woven items.

Jicalpextle: Lacquered gourd bowl, hand-painted with floral designs, a specialty of Chiapa de Corzo, Chiapas. Now expensive and rarely used in Isthmus fiestas.

Juaneca: Woman native of San Juan Evangelista.

Ladrillo: Adobe brick.

Limosna: Woman's ritual contribution, usually $3.

Machismo: Excessive concern with proving one's maleness.

Material: Products necessary for quality house construction, including adobe, tile, and plaster.

Mayordomo: Sponsor of fiesta.

Mazorca: Unhusked ear of mature maize.

Mestizo: Person bearing national culture, usually speaking national language only, having no known or recognizable ethnic ties.

Mezcal: Alcoholic beverage made from maguey.

Mixa guétu: Death rites, literally "mass for the dead."

Mole: Red sauce of chile and other condiments, usually containing bits of turkey or other meat.

Monte (el):   Literally "the bush," that part of the land not cultivated.

Municipio: Smallest political unit of the Republic of Mexico, somewhat similar to U.S. county.

Muy cerrado: Inhospitable to outsiders, very secretive and inwardly oriented.

Nixtamal: Maize soaked in lime water, ready to be ground into coarse dough (masa).

Norte (el):   The prevalent strong north wind.

Novena: Catholic mourning period.

Novio: Sweetheart or bridegroom.

Ojo: Evil eye.

Olan: Deep white-pleated lace flounce at bottom of the *traje* skirt.

Olla: Pottery jar.

Padre: Catholic priest.

Padrino: Godparent of a child in baptism, communion, or marriage.

Palo: Wood stick or club.

Palacio: City hall.

Panteon (el):   The cemetery. Major Isthmus towns have several.

Partera: Midwife.

Paseando: Strolling idly about for pleasure and recreation.

Paseo: Promenade around the central square, a traditional courting mechanism of Spain and Latin America.

Pasta: Macaroni and other wheat dough products of Italian origin.

Peso: Mexican currency valued at approximately 8 cents U.S. in 1966–1967.

Petate: Woven sleeping mat.

Plazita: Neighborhood or barrio market places.

Politico: A politician or one who has political ambitions or one who trys to maneuver people and his social position to best advantage.

Por civil: By civil ceremony.

Por los dos lados: By both sides; married by both civil and religious rites.

Por robar: Marriage by elopement, by "robbing."

Pozol: Sweet, cornmeal-based drink.

Presidente: Elected head of the local municipio government, an office somewhat analogous to U.S. mayor.

Promesa: Vow to a saint.

Pueblo libre: Politically autonomous pueblo.

Pueblo rebelde: A rebellious town or community.

Puesto: Market stall.

Rebozo: Woman's shawl.

Redila: Open stock truck with high slat sides and endgate.

Refresco: Cold beverage, often with fruit base.

Rezadora: Woman prayer leader.

Salsa: Sauce, usually made from chiles and often containing tomatoes.

Santa mesa: Household shrine.

Santa mesa (men's):   The "saint's table" where men pay their ceremonial fees at fiestas.

Señora: Matron, a married or widowed woman.

Serrano: A person native to the sierra.

Sierra: Mountainous region.

Sin cultura: "Without culture," lacking in social refinement.

Solar: The house site and all structures thereon.

Soldado: Soldier.

Susto: Fright.

Tardecita: Late afternoon and early evening.

Templo: Temple, a non-Catholic religious structure.

Terrenos: farm lands.

Terrenos de labor: Gardens, orchards, and small fields requiring intensive care.

Tesis: Thesis, a word familiar to informants because it is a requirement for a teaching credential in the federal educational system.

Tia: Aunt.

Tiendita: Little store.

Todos Santos: All Souls' Day.

Torito: Young ox.

Torta: Small cake.

Tortillera: A woman who makes or sells tortillas.

Totopo: An oven-baked tortilla, specialty of San Juan Evangelista.

Totopera: A woman who makes or sells totopos.

Traje: The hand-embroidered velvet huipil and skirt worn by women on ceremonial occasions. In San Juan Evangelista it is known as *Traje Tehuana*.

Tristeza: Sadness.

Turista: Tourist.

Ultramarinos: Imported food items.

Urbano: Municipal bus.

Vallista: A person from the Valley of Oaxaca.

Vela: Literally "candle" but referring to a festival of one evening's duration associated with a longer fiesta.

Vestido: Woman's dress, used only to refer to street-length European-type dress.

Viajera: Traveling woman vendor.

Xuana: Principal; barrio headman, formerly a politico-religious office but now only religious.

References

Aswad, Barbara C., 1967, "Key and Peripheral Roles of Noble Women in a Middle Eastern Plains Village." *Anthropological Quarterly* 40:139–152.

Brown, Judith, 1970, "A Note on the Division of Labor by Sex." *American Anthropologist* 72:1073–1078.

Cajigas Langner, Alberto, 1954, *Monografia de Tehuantepec*. Mexico: Imprenta Manuel Leon Sanchez, S.C.L.

VIII Censo General de Poblacion, 1960, Tomo II, Mexico, published in 1963.

Chagnon, Napoleon A., 1968, *Yanomamö: The Fierce People*. New York: Holt, Rinehart and Winston, Inc.

Covarrubias, Miguel, 1954, *Mexico South: The Isthmus of Tehuantepec*. New York: Alfred A. Knopf. First printing 1946.

Delgado, Agustin, 1961, "La secuencia arqueologica en el Istmo de Tehuantepec," in *Los Mayas del Sur y sus Relaciones con Los Nahuas Meridionales*. VIII Mesa Redonda (1959), Sociedad Mexicana de Antropologia. Mexico.

Elkin, A.P., 1950, Introduction to *Aboriginal Woman* by Phyllis Kayberry. New York: Humanities Press, Inc.

Elmendorf, Mary L., 1971, "The Role of Women as Agents for Peaceful Social Change." Unpublished paper read at 12th World Conference of the Society for International Development, Ottawa, Canada, May 17.

Forster, James R., 1953, "Notas Sobre la Arqueologia de Tehuantepec." *Anales de Instituto Nacional de Antropologia e Historia* 7:77–100. Mexico.

Foster, George M., 1961, "The Dyadic Contract: A Model for the Social Structure of a Peasant Village." *American Anthropologist* 63:1173–1192.

———, 1965, "Peasant Society and the Image of Limited Good." *American Anthropologist* 67:2.

Friedl, Ernestine, 1967, "The Position of Women: Appearance and Reality." *Anthropological Quarterly* 40:97–108.

Gay, Jose Antonio, 1950, Historia de Oaxaca. Vol. 2, Tomo Primero, 3rd ed. Mexico. First printing 1881.

Goodale, Jane, 1970, *Tiwi Wives*, AES Monograph #50. Seattle: University of Washington Press.

Harris, Marvin, 1971, *Culture, Man, and Nature*. New York: Thomas Y. Crowell Company.

Hart, C.W.M., and Arnold Pilling, 1960, *The Tiwi of North Australia*. New York: Holt, Rinehart and Winston, Inc.

Iturribarria, Jorge Fernando, 1960, "Yagul: Mestizo Product of Mixtecs and Zapotecs." Boletin No. 17, Estudios Oaxaqueños, John Paddoc, ed. Mexico.

Lee, Richard B., 1968, "What Hunters Do For a Living or How to Make Out on Scarce Resources," in Richard Lee and Irven DeVore, eds., *Man the Hunter*. Chicago: Aldine Publishing Co.

———, and Irven DeVore, eds., 1968, *Man the Hunter*. Chicago: Aldine Publishing Co.

Mintz, Sidney, 1969, "Review of *Peasants* by Eric R. Wolf." *American Anthropologist* 71:1136–1139.

Mintz, Sidney W., and Eric R. Wolf, 1950, "An Analysis of Ritual Co-Parenthood." *Southwestern Journal of Anthropology* 341–364. Bobbs-Merrill Reprint A-159.

Riegelhaupt, Joyce F., 1967, "Saloio Women: An Analysis of Informal and Formal

Political and Economic Roles of Portuguese Peasant Women." *Anthropological Quarterly* 40:97–108.

Spindler, George, and Louise Spindler, 1970, "Fieldwork Among the Menomini," in George D. Spindler, ed., *Being an Anthropologist: Fieldwork in Eleven Cultures*. New York: Holt, Rinehart and Winston, Inc.

Torres de Lagunas, Juan de, 1580, "Descripcion de Teguantepec," in Vargas Rea, ed., *Biblioteca Aportacion Historica*, 1958, Mexico.

Wolf, Eric R., 1966, "Kinship, Friendship, and Patron-Client Relations in Complex Societies," in M. Banton, ed., *The Social Anthropology of Complex Societies*, ASA Mon. 4. New York: Frederick A. Praeger, Inc.

———, 1967, "Closed Corporate Peasant Communities in Mesoamerica and Central Java," in Jack Potter et al., ed., *Peasant Society: A Reader*, Boston: Little, Brown & Co.

Recommended reading

Works on Isthmus Zapotecs and other Peasant Communities of Mexico selected for readability, recency, or particular relevance to this study are:

Covarrubias, Miguel, 1954, *Mexico South: The Isthmus of Tehuantepec.* New York: Alfred A. Knopf. A colorful, somewhat romanticized account of Isthmus Zapotecs is part of a treatment of the entire area, including notes on several other ethnic groups. The author was a famous Mexican artist who developed a great interest in pre-Columbian artifacts, especially those of the Olmec style.

Foster, George M., 1967, *Tzintzuntzan: Mexican Peasants in a Changing World.* Boston: Little, Brown & Company.
A readable account of a mestisized Tarascan community on the shores of Lake Pátzcuaro.

Kearney, Michael, 1972, *The Winds of Ixtepeji.* New York: Holt, Rinehart, and Winston, Inc.
The perception of reality in a Zapotec community in the Valley of Oaxaca.

Leslie, Charles, 1960, *Now We Are Civilized: A study of the World View of the Zapotec Indians of Mitla, Oaxaca.* Detroit: Wayne State University Press.

Litzler, B. N., 1968, *Women of San Blas Atempa: An Analysis of the Economic Role of Isthmus Zapotec Women in Relation to Family and Community.* Unpublished dissertation, University of Michigan. University Microfilms, Ann Arbor, Mich.
Centers on women's market activities, types of selling, products, modes of operation, income derived from selling, and other details of the household and market economy.

Madsen, William, 1960, *The Virgin's Children: Life in an Aztec Village Today.* Austin: University of Texas Press.
The study of a Nahua community of central Mexico.

Parsons, Elsie Clews, 1936, *Mitla, Town of the Souls.* Chicago: University of Chicago Press.
Parsons' study remains useful for an understanding of Valley Zapotec culture as it was 40 years ago. The Appendix E is especially helpful on trade goods and trade routes.

Turner, Paul, 1972, *The Highland Chontal.* New York: Holt, Rinehart and Winston, Inc.
Interesting because the Highland Chontal are neighbors of the Isthmus Zapotecs geographically but there is very little social interaction between the two distinct ethnic groups. Also worth reading for the insight it affords of a value system which is incompatible with Protestantism.

Relevant readings for insight into women's roles generally and in specific cultures are:

Brown, Judith, 1970, "A Note on the Division of Labor by Sex." *American Anthropologist* 72:1073–1078.

Dupire, Marguerite, 1963, "The Position of Women in a Pastoral Society," in Denise Pauline, ed., *Women of Tropical Africa.* Berkeley: University of California Press.

Friedl, Ernestine, 1967, "The Position of Women: Appearance and Reality." *Anthropological Quarterly* 40:97–108.
    Women's roles in a Greek peasant community.
Lebeuf, Annie, 1963, "The Role of Women in the Political Organization of African Societies," in Denise Paulme, ed., *Women of Tropical Africa*. Berkeley: University of California Press.
    Traces the history of women in African political systems from precolonial times and suggests that women's formal political roles often suffered under colonialism.
Mintz, Sidney, 1971, "Men, Women, and Trade." *Comparative Studies in Society and History* 13:247–269.
    Discusses women's marketing roles in Africa, the Carribean, and other areas and ways in which "modernization" of underdeveloped economies may be detrimental to women and women's trading activities.
Riegelhaupt, Joyce F., 1967, "Saloio Women: An Analysis of Informal and Formal Political and Economic Roles of Portuguese Peasant Women." *Anthropological Quarterly* 40:109–126.